AN EXTRAORDINARY POLITICAL MOMENT — AN EXTRAORDINARY OPPORTUNITY

Nearly everyone would agree that this year's presidential election cycle has taken surprising turns. In the summer of 2015, many assumed that Hillary Clinton and Jeb Bush would be the inevitable respective nominees of the Democratic and Republican parties.[1] Both were establishment figures and part of competing political dynasties with access to extraordinary financial resources. As many observers noted, the nominations of these leaders felt more like a coronation than an election.[2] Yet several political outsiders who played the game by very different rules ran campaigns that defied all expectations. Bush's candidacy faded quickly in a large field of newcomers that included Ted Cruz, Marco Rubio, Donald J. Trump, and others. Clinton's candidacy faced a relentless challenge from a surprisingly revitalized social democratic Left led by Vermont Senator Bernie Sanders. By the end of July 2016, two players had clinched the Republican and Democratic nominations, even though both Donald Trump and Hillary Clinton continued to be viewed with suspicion by large blocs of their respective parties. Something new seemed to be going on in American presidential politics. These candidates and the way they conducted their campaigns suggested that this was not politics-as-usual.

---

1 See, e.g., Eric Ham, "Clinton has inevitability, but Bush has the Electoral College." *The Hill.* April 3, 2015. Available at http://thehill.com/blogs/pundits-blog/presidential-campaign/237802-clinton-has-inevitability-but-bush-has-the-electoral. Accessed September 30, 2016.

2 See, e.g., Perry Bacon Jr., "Influential Republicans Wary of Bush Coronation." NBC News. February 27, 2015. Available at http://www.nbcnews.com/politics/elections/influential-republicans-wary-bush-coronation-n314396. Accessed September 30, 2016; Philip Rucker and Ed O'Keefe, "Clinton, Bush struggle to shed dynasty labels during holiday parades in N.H." *The Washington Post.* July 4, 2015. Available at https://www.washingtonpost.com/politics/clinton-and-bush-struggle-to-shed-dynasty-labels-in-nh-parades/2015/07/04/93173942-2285-11e5-84d5-eb37ee8eaa61_story.html. Accessed September 30, 2016.

So what was going on? Did we witness a "one-off" anomaly in the history of U.S. presidential elections? Or did the way the race unfolded signal a fundamental transformation of our larger political culture and institutions?

Our instincts tell us that the often chaotic, anti-establishment theme of this election season signals a culmination of trends that have been developing for several decades. What exactly are those changes? How deep do they go? What segments of the American population are most implicated in these changes? And finally, what do they mean for American democracy?

This extraordinary moment also presents an extraordinary opportunity to explore what is going on beneath the surface of American political life. And that is precisely what we set out to do in our *2016 Survey of American Political Culture*. Based on 1,904 telephone interviews with a nationally representative sample of American adults (oversampling for African-Americans, Hispanics, and the well-educated), this survey provides a granular, empirically rich picture of some of the underlying dynamics of American political culture today, dynamics that are likely to shape democratic life through the early years of the twenty-first century.

Politics and Political Culture: The Critical Difference

The Institute for Advanced Studies in Culture takes a distinctive approach in its work and in this particular task. Most public opinion surveys tend to focus on the latest attitudes and opinions concerning a small number of issues. The value of such surveys is in communicating what the public thinks about a candidate or how they would likely vote at a particular moment in time. Within days, those findings become old news. The surveys sponsored by the Institute, however, focus on the political culture that is the substrate of such political attitudes and behavior. Put another way, we focus on the climate rather than the weather.

Mutatis mutandis, in popular culture politics is viewed as the daily, ongoing contest for power. So horse race journalism typically attends to the latest changes in political fortune: Who's up, who's down, who's gaining, who's losing, what did they say today and will it be contradicted by something they say tomorrow, and so on. By contrast, the Institute is preeminently concerned with the cultural context in which political contests takes place. This context includes the ideals, beliefs, values, symbols, stories, and public rituals that either bind or separate people, but always direct them in political action. Political culture provides the boundaries of political legitimacy and the horizons of political possibility. Political activity in large part emanates from political culture, reflecting that culture's deepest values and beliefs. Political action, in turn, both reinforces and subtly reshapes the political culture.

The everyday politics of a society may change and change significantly, but the normative context — the political culture — of a society tends to change very slowly. When it does, the changes are of great consequence. Changes that take place within political culture portend much about the future ordering of public life.

The *2016 Survey of American Political Culture* seeks in particular to understand how electoral politics relate to questions concerning the fragmentation and polarization of American civic life, the erosion of the moral foundations for citizenship, the coarsening of public discourse, the political significance of new religious, racial, ethnic, and class divisions, and the loss of legitimacy for key public institutions.

Public opinion surveys can touch upon only certain kinds of information and must rely upon self-reporting. Though they can never provide the final word on any topic, they are an important component in any broad analysis of political culture. This survey seeks to bridge the empirical and theoretical, and to enable us to speak, even if provisionally, with greater care and specificity about the "climatological" political and cultural changes taking place across America. By exploring these matters in some depth, we hope that this survey will enrich our understanding of the current political milieu and help us to address more effectively the serious challenges facing both our democracy and the culture that sustains it.

James Davison Hunter
LaBrosse-Levinson Distinguished Professor
of Religion, Culture and Social Theory
Institute for Advanced Studies in Culture

Carl Desportes Bowman
Senior Fellow & Director of Survey Research
Institute for Advanced Studies in Culture

CONTENTS

II: The Contours of Disaffection

III: The New Culture Wars

IV: An Afterword on Late-Stage Democracy

Appendix

THE CONTESTED MEANING OF THE 2016 PRESIDENTIAL ELECTION

There are at least two competing narratives about the 2016 presidential election.

The first and conventional narrative is that while the primary season was at times entertaining and at times alarming, this was an election like any other. Every four years, America goes through a ritual of electing (or reelecting) a president. In 2016 we simply reenacted that important democratic ritual. To be sure, the candidacies of Donald Trump and, to a lesser extent, Bernie Sanders, and still others through the primary season, introduced surprising new elements into the process. Yet American democracy is big enough and stable enough to absorb those novelties without their affecting the core governing principles and practices of the system and of the party apparatus that champions those principles and practices.

In the framework of this narrative, the 2016 *Survey of American Political Culture* found that as of the last weeks of August (and still in the post-convention honeymoon), the establishment candidate, Hillary Clinton, held a safe lead (51%) over the political outsider, Donald Trump (35%), "if the Presidential election were being held today." These figures shifted throughout September and are likely to change more in the final weeks of the campaign.

It is important to note that neither candidate enjoys strong favorability among the general public. Roughly 57 percent of Americans view Clinton unfavorably and even more — 70 percent — view Trump unfavorably. These figures are precisely comparable to many other surveys tracking these attitudes,[3] which collectively reveal a decided lack of enthusiasm among the majority of voters for either one of the candidates. Many Americans, it would seem, prefer "none of the above."[4] Indeed, in the post-convention context in which his candidacy posed no threat, Bernie Sanders enjoyed a favorability rating of 59 percent.

Figure 1: Opinions of Political Figures

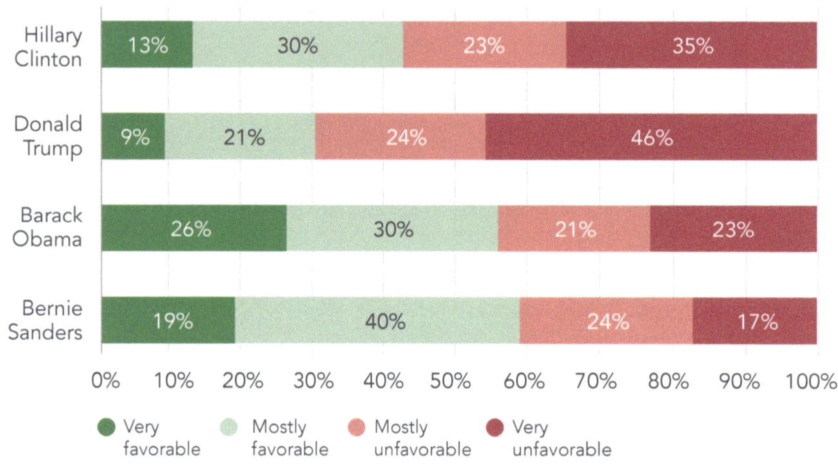

Even in the framework of this narrative, the survey unearthed patterns in American public opinion that lay bare a chasm of fundamentally different worldviews. For example,

- Of those who say they will vote for Clinton, 73 percent agree that "the government should do more to improve the lives of ordinary Americans," compared to 24 percent of those voting for Trump.[5]

3 http://www.realclearpolitics.com/epolls/other/trump_favorableunfavorable-5493.html and http://www.realclearpolitics.com/epolls/other/clinton_favorableunfavorable-1131.html.

4 See, Janet Hook, "Growing Faction of Voters Say 'Neither of the Above.'" *The Wall Street Journal.* July 14, 2016. Available at http://blogs.wsj.com/washwire/2016/07/14/growing-faction-of-voters-say-neither-of-the-above. Accessed September 30, 2016.

5 This partisan disparity is echoed in other surveys; the Pew Research Center, for instance, reports (http://www.pewglobal.org/files/2013/01/Stokes_Bruce_NAF_Public_Attitudes_1_2013.pdf) that between 1987 and 2012, Democrats have consistently been more likely than Republicans to agree that "It's the government's responsibility to take care of people who can't take care of themselves" and that "The government should guarantee every citizen enough to eat and a place to sleep."

- Of those saying they will vote for Trump, 77 percent say that they were in favor of "building a wall across the border between the US and Mexico," compared to only 8 percent of those voting for Clinton.[6]

- In a similar vein, 70 percent of all Trump supporters favor "banning entry to all Muslims until we better understand the threat to our country," while 82 percent of all Clinton supporters oppose that policy.[7]

- When asked "if more Americans legally carried weapons in public" would it make our nation safer or more dangerous, eight out of ten Clinton supporters (79%) said it would make the nation more dangerous, while seven out of ten Trump supporters (68%) said it would make the nation safer.[8]

- Not least, 85 percent of all Trump supporters were in favor of "repealing the Affordable Care Act," while 73 percent of all Clinton supporters opposed that idea.[9]

---

6 This finding is in line with a PRRI/Brookings Institute poll (http://www.prri.org/research/prri-brookings-immigration-report) during the 2016 primary campaign; it found 66 percent of all Republicans and 82 percent of Trump supporters in favor of a wall on the Mexican border, compared to only 23 percent of Democrats.

7 The same PRRI/Brookings Institute poll found 64 percent of all Republicans and 77% of Trump supporters in favor of such a ban, compared to 23 percent of Democrats. The rejection of this policy is also worth considering alongside the results of the 2003 *Difference and Democracy* survey, in which 88 percent of respondents agreed that "the U.S. armed forces should continue the fight against terror until all serious threats have been eliminated." These findings suggest that Americans see the fight against terrorism as a predominately military-oriented effort, not one that involves sweeping changes to the civic traditions of American pluralism and policies vis-à-vis immigrants and tourists. Despite their real concerns about terrorism, it remains true that, as Carl Bowman wrote in his article "The Evidence for Empire" (*The Hedgehog Review*, Spring 2003), "Most Americans not only acknowledge, but welcome, the increasing cultural and religious pluralism that has penetrated even the most remote areas of the country."

8 The finding of polarization on this issue echoes a 2015 Gallup poll (http://www.gallup.com/poll/186263/majority-say-concealed-weapons-safer.aspx), in which 56 percent of all respondents said that the country would be safer if more Americans carried concealed weapons and 41 percent said it would be less safe.

9 Here again, the finding of stark divides between Clinton and Trump supporters can explain broader polarization on the issue. A 2015 Gallup poll (http://www.gallup.com/poll/184079/americans-views-healthcare-law-improve.aspx) found that 48 percent of respondents disapproved of the Affordable Care Act, while 47 percent approved.

These are far from minor differences. Symbolically, the Clinton and Trump candidacies crystallize two fundamentally different pictures of the world. So even if the conventional narrative is true, there are aspects of this election that confirm its unusual nature.

An Alternative Narrative

The second narrative offers an alternative interpretation of this election. Using the actual language of contemporary political commentary, this opposing interpretation holds that this election reveals "the failure of the liberal mainstream"[10] and even the "end of liberalism." To be sure, "American democracy has been able to thrive with unprecedented stability over the last couple of centuries...but it is not immortal." Our politics, it is said, gives expression to a "late-stage democracy" and, in fact, ours may now be a "democracy in name only" making "America ripe for tyranny."[11] As to Trump, it has been claimed that his candidacy "embodies how great republics meet their end,"[12] and has brought us to "a Joe McCarthy moment."[13] Even more ominously, we are to wonder if the demagoguery and authoritarian rhetoric we are hearing from the Right and Left has brought us to "the West's Weimar moment."[14]

This narrative is admittedly more speculative. Its confirmation depends on how things turn out. The fact is, each narrative is plausible in its own way and, in our view, it is far too early to tell which holds the greater truth. James

---

10 Jochen Bittner, "Is This the West's Weimar Moment?" *The New York Times*. May 31, 2016. Available at http://www.nytimes.com/2016/05/31/opinion/is-this-the-wests-weimar-moment.html. Accessed September 30, 2016. In our current political milieu, it should be noted that "liberal mainstream" here encompasses administrations from both political parties over the past half century.

11 Andrew Sullivan, "America has never been so ripe for tyranny." *New York Magazine*. May 1, 2016. Available at http://nymag.com/daily/intelligencer/2016/04/america-tyranny-donald-trump. html. Accessed September 30, 2016.

12 Martin Wolf, "Donald Trump Embodies How Great Republics Meet Their End." *Financial Times*. March 1, 2016. Available at https://www.ft.com/content/743d91b8-df8d-11e5-b67f-a61732c1d025. Accessed September 30, 2016.

13 David Brooks, "If Not Trump, What?" *The New York Times*. April 29, 2016. Available at http:// www.nytimes.com/2016/04/29/opinion/if-not-trump-what.html. Accessed September 30, 2016.

14 Bittner, "Is This the West's Weimar Moment?"

Madison observed that democracies "have ever been spectacles of turbulence and contention"; So maybe there is nothing to worry about. Yet in the same breath, Madison also noted that democracies "have in general been as short in their lives as they have been violent in their deaths." Is the 2016 election a protracted near-death experience?

The Setting

We live in a time of world-historical change marked by, among other things, extensive social disruption. At the heart of this transformation are the global flows of money, information, technology and people that constitute economic, political and cultural globalization. Within this we see a rise in the power and transnational authority of international corporations, nongovernmental organizations and terrorist groups, and a destabilization of the longstanding international order. Despite relative steadiness in financial markets, this is also a time of economic stagnation in wide swaths of the global economy and political instability within nation-states around the world, not least in the developing world. These economic and political matters are complicated further by massive immigration.

We live in a world whose boundaries are in flux. This is evident in various parts of public life: in the sectors of the economy that are expanding and contracting, in the patterns of immigration that accompany political and economic disruption, in the realm of education in response to ever-changing economic needs, in the technology of knowledge and communication, and in the shuffling of prestige and privilege. It is equally true in the private realm, where values, beliefs, the nature of family, intimacy, and community are all being challenged and reconfigured.

Though corruption can be found in all sectors — and even in places where corruption doesn't exist — political, financial, corporate and cultural establishments have failed to lead effectively in ways that seek the flourishing of everyone.

With all of this has come popular frustration, disappointment and anger, particularly among those who have neither the educational credentials nor the cultural and economic skills to navigate the demands of increasingly cosmopolitan, global realities. Against this backdrop, it is not surprising that we see a rise of popular demand to "make things right again." Nor is it surprising that we would witness around the world the reappearance of authoritarian figures[15] and messages responding to that demand, promising clarity and control in a world that is infinitely opaque and exceptionally difficult to manage. The efforts of figures like Cruz, Sanders and Trump to harness that popular disaffection with a changing world and the governing elite is not isolated, but part of a larger global pattern.[16]

15 Marine Le Pen in France, Vladimir Putin in Russia, Silvio Berlusconi in Italy, Joseph Zuma in South Africa and Thaksin Shinawatra in Thailand.

16 Indeed, "Make America Great Again" was a prominent shibboleth of the Reagan-Bush campaign in 1980 and also peppered the speeches of Bill Clinton's 1992 presidential run.

I

THE ONGOING CRISIS OF LEGITIMACY

Times of change, then, are times of confusion — and worry and fear alike. Inevitably, there are political ramifications. But even before they take political form, the ramifications are *pre-political*; that is, uncertainty, worry, fear, and frustration play out in people's dispositions toward their governing institutions and leaders. Politics invariably is an artifact of these dynamics; it is an extension and reflection of these dispositions.

America: Affection and Disquiet

How do Americans perceive their nation and their place in it?

First, Americans love their country and hold it in the highest regard. Nearly half (47%) of all Americans believe that America "is the greatest country in the world, better than all other countries"[17] and nearly as many (43%) see America as "a great country, but so are certain other countries." Eight of ten (81%) also agree that "America is an exceptional nation with a special responsibility to lead the world."[18] Overwhelmingly (93%), they also describe themselves as patriotic. Indeed, most (57%) describe themselves as "*very* patriotic." There is variation here, but more in tone than substance.[19]

---

17 This does, however, represent a decline from 1996, when 55 percent of respondents to the Institute for Advanced Studies in Culture's *State of Disunion* survey reported that the United States was the greatest country in the world.

18 This finding echoes that of the Institute for Advanced Studies in Culture's 2003 survey *Difference and Democracy*, in which 79 percent of respondents agreed that "America must lead the world into the 21st century."

19 Looking more closely we see some significant variation, not least among the different generations, in the intensity of their views. Only 29 percent of all Millennials see the U.S. as the

Yet despite this abundance of admiration and patriotism, the mood in the nation is not positive. Indeed, *less* than 5 percent of all respondents believe that America is "strongly improving." Instead, half of all Americans believe it is in decline, some (26%) believe it is "strongly declining" and the rest (23%) believe it is moderately declining. About a third of the population (33%) believe that the nation is "holding steady." There is a remarkable continuity here over the past two decades.[20] Whether in decline or not, more than half of all respondents (58%) agree that "the American way of life," whatever they understand that to mean, "is rapidly disappearing."[21]

As they assess their own circumstances, Americans are divided in how they see the trajectory of their own lot in life over the last 25 years: About a third (36%) say their life has gotten worse, a third (36%) say it has improved, and about a quarter (27%) see it as holding steady.[22] Americans are similarly divided in how they imagine their future: 36% better, 29% the same, and 35% worse. As they assess their "current financial situation," Americans are split down the middle: Half see their financial situation as good (42%) or excellent (9%) and half see it has fair (36%) or poor (14%).[23] With some

greatest country in the world compared to 57 percent of all of the Baby Boomers and 67 percent of the Silent Generation. In a similar way, one-third of the Millennials (33%) see themselves as "very patriotic" compared to three-fourths of the Boomers (72%) and Silent Generation (77%). The 57 percent of respondents describing themselves as "very patriotic" represent an increase from the 51 percent who did so in the 2003 *Difference and Democracy* survey.

20 Belief in the country's experience of decline has not grown significantly since 1996, when the *State of Disunion* survey found that 22 percent of respondents saw a strong decline in the United States and another 30 percent saw a moderate decline.

21 This echoes the findings of a Quinnipiac University survey from earlier this year (https://www.qu.edu/news-and-events/quinnipiac-university-poll/national/release-detail?ReleaseID=2340), in which 57 percent of respondents agreed that "America has lost its identity," and a PRRI/Brookings Institute survey from this year (http://www.prri.org/research/prri-brookings-immigration-report/), which found that 50 percent of respondents agreed that the American culture and way of life have mostly changed for the worse since the 1950s.

22 While respondents' evaluations of their personal life circumstances are divided, they are, on balance, more optimistic than their evaluations of the broader state of the nation. This finding echoes a longstanding trend in survey research, discussed at length in *The Confidence Gap* (New York: The Free Press, 1983) by Seymour Martin Lipset and William Schneider: Americans typically offer more positive assessments of their own personal circumstances than of the country as a whole.

23 This finding is roughly comparable with that of a Quinnipiac University survey from earlier this year (https://www.qu.edu/news-and-events/quinnipiac-university-poll/national/release-detail?ReleaseID=2340), which found that 57 percent of respondents agreed that they were

minor but important exceptions, all of these views are held fairly consistently across many demographic groupings.[24]

A Faltering Establishment

The source of the general disquiet in the nation, then, does not seem to be a reflection of personal circumstances, as varied as they are. Rather, the disquiet is rooted in their perception of the governing institutions of the nation and their leadership. It is important to note that it isn't American democracy *per se* that is the problem. On this point, 84 percent agree that they "are proud to live under our American system of government."[25] Rather, the consensus of disaffection draws from the perception that the dominant institutions of American society and their leadership have failed to deliver on their promises.

Disaffection With the Government

Nearly two-thirds (64%) of the American public have little to no confidence that "the government in Washington" will actually solve the problems it sets its mind to. We asked this question in 1996 and found much the same — the figure was 60 percent two decades ago.[26] The difference is that, 20 years on, the attitudes have hardened: Where 21 percent of the American population said they had no confidence at all in 1996, that figure jumped to 30 percent in 2016.

The cynicism about the government is astonishing. To give a sense of how deep it is, consider the fact that the overwhelming majority of Americans (88%) believe that "political events these days seem more like theater or entertainment than like something to be taken seriously." Here, too, public opinion has hardened: In 1996, 79 percent agreed with that statement,

---

"falling further and further behind economically," while 42 percent disagreed.

24 That said, whites and Baby Boomers generally tend to see more decline in the country and in their lot in life than African-Americans and Hispanics, and thus a slightly larger percentage of African-Americans and Hispanics tend to see America (and their own circumstances) on an upward trajectory. As expected, the assessment of personal financial situation varies considerably across educational and income groups.

25 There is, though, an alarming 16 percent of the population who disagree.

26 In fact, this question has been asked consistently over 25 years and the patterns are nearly identical.

31 percent agreeing completely.[27] Today, 45 percent of the American public completely agree with this view.

The concern Americans have is neither abstract nor negligible to them. Their suspicions are broadly, if not universally, held: Just over half (56%) of all respondents today, for example, agree that "the government in Washington threatens the freedom of ordinary Americans."[28]

Americans are ambivalent about the apparatus of both leading parties. On the one hand, nearly 60 percent (57%) of all self-identified Republicans and nearly 80 percent (78%) of all self-described Democrats say that their respective parties "represent their own views of how the government should operate." On the other hand, 63 percent also believe that "what Americans really need is a new political party because the current two-party system isn't working."[29] Over half of all Democrats (53%) and Republicans (56%) hold this view, but three out of four (74%) of the growing number of Independents are especially adamant about this. The expansion of Independents during the last 20 years itself attests to the weakening of the two-party system. Our 1996 Survey found 31 percent identifying themselves as Independents. By this year, it had risen to 42 percent, more than identify with either of the major parties. All of this points to the declining credibility of the political parties as carriers of the claims, aspirations and, in turn, the shared identity and solidarity they once provided.

Disaffection With its Leaders

The real problem for the majority of Americans is how the government in Washington and beyond is actually managed. Here the special ire of the

---

27 In 2003, the *Difference and Democracy* survey found that comparatively fewer respondents (69%) agreed with the statement, with 22 percent agreeing completely.

28 Here again, we find continuity; the 2003 *Difference and Democracy* survey found that 57 percent of respondents either completely or mostly agreed that "the federal government controls too much of our daily lives."

29 Gallup has tracked interest in a third political party over time (http://www.gallup.com/poll/185891/majority-maintain-need-third-major-party.aspx). They find that the percentage of respondents saying that a third party is needed generally fluctuates within the 50-60 percent range, though there has been a recent uptick that is in line with our findings.

American public is directed toward the political leaders in the power centers of government. Consider:

- 90 percent — nine of ten Americans — believe that "most politicians are more interested in winning elections than in doing what is right."[30]

- 73 percent agree that "most elected officials don't care what people like me think."[31]

- Over 70 percent believe that while the "system of government is good... the people running it are incompetent."[32]

- 63 percent agree that "people like me don't have any say about what the government does."[33]

And 45 percent agree that "the police and law enforcement unfairly target racial and ethnic minorities," though among African-Americans, the number swells to 83 percent, and among Hispanics, the figure is 56 percent.[34]

---

30 This is an increase from 79 percent in the 1996 *State of Disunion* survey, 82 percent in the 2000 *Politics of Character* survey, and 84 percent in the 2003 *Difference and Democracy* survey.

31 Almost as large a share of respondents, 69 percent agreed with this statement in the 1996 *State of Disunion* survey. A 2016 Quinnipiac survey (https://www.qu.edu/news-and-events/quinnipiac-university-poll/national/release-detail?ReleaseID=2340) found that respondents who supported Donald Trump in the Republican primaries were more likely to agree that "public officials don't care much what people like me think" than were respondents supporting other Republican candidates or a Democratic candidate.

32 This represents only a slight increase from the 1996 *State of Disunion* survey, which found that 66 percent agreed with the statement. However, the uptick in those who "completely agree" with the statement is more prominent; 29 percent completely agreed in 2016, compared to only 16 percent in 1996. It also represents an uptick from 2003, when the *Difference and Democracy* survey found that 11 percent of respondents completely agreed and 37 percent mostly agreed.

33 Sixty percent of respondents agreed with this statement in the 1996 *State of Disunion* survey, and 57 percent agreed in the 2000 *Politics of Character* survey.

34 These findings echo those of a 2015 Gallup survey (http://www.gallup.com/poll/184511/blacks-divided-whether-police-treat-minorities-fairly.aspx). It found that while 78 percent of non-Hispanic whites felt that police in their area treated racial minorities fairly, only 71 percent of Hispanics and 52 percent of African-Americans agreed.

Figure 2: Opinions of Political Leaders

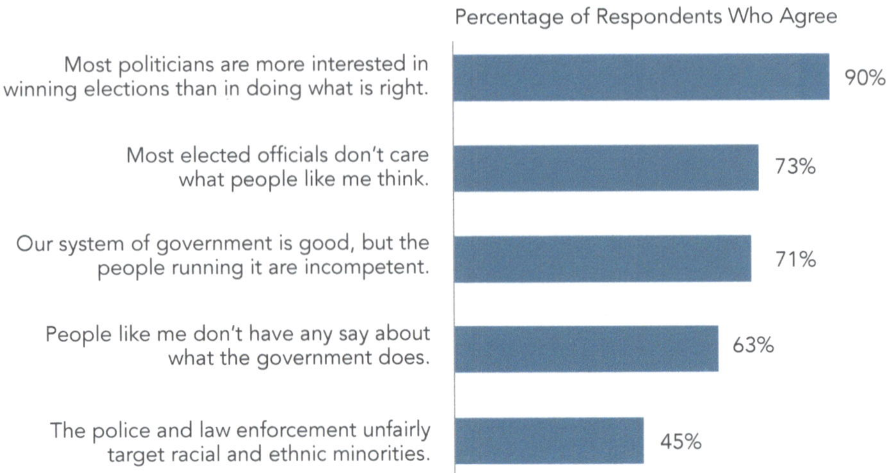

The problem is not only with the political elites, but also with leaders in business, finance, the media and beyond. Thus, 84 percent agree that "Wall Street and big business in our country often profit at the expense of ordinary Americans." Seventy-three percent of all Americans believe that "our economic system is rigged in favor of the wealthiest Americans." These findings reinforce a longstanding distrust toward the motives and influences of big business.[35]

As much as these institutions come in for criticism, so too do their leaders. Sixty-two percent of the American public agrees that "the leaders in American corporations, media, universities and technology care little about the lives of most Americans." By the same ratio (62%), the public is convinced that "the most educated and successful people in America are more interested in serving themselves than in serving the common good."[36]

---

35 There is a long history of Americans voicing skepticism regarding the willingness of big business to conduct itself in ways that would benefit the average person. Lipset and Schneider report in *The Confidence Gap* that in 1981, a Harris poll found that only 30 percent of respondents gave a positive evaluation of "the job American business is doing to solve our economic problems." They also report that, in four surveys conducted by Cambridge Reports, Inc. between 1975 and 1977, between 69 and 79 percent of respondents agreed that "Big business doesn't care whether I live or die, only that somebody buys what they have to sell."

36 This skepticism of elites has deep historical roots. In their book, *The Confidence Gap*, Lipset

Figure 3: Opinions of Leaders of Other Institutions

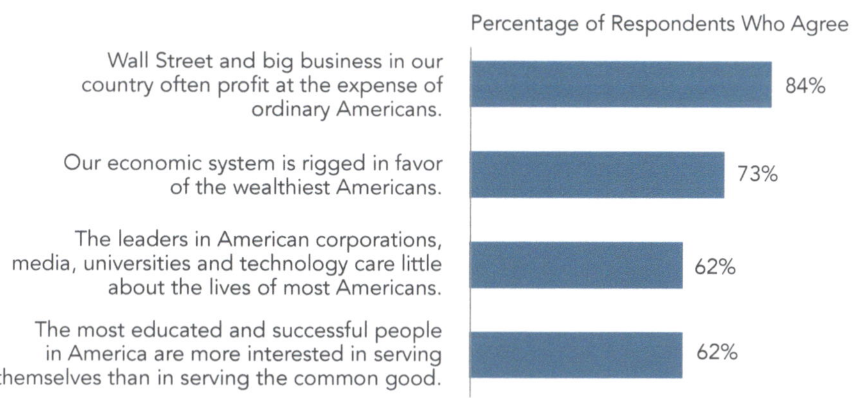

"Political Correctness" and the Problem of Truth in Contemporary American Democracy

One of the problems perceived by a wide swath of the American public is the issue of political correctness. Nearly three out of four Americans (73%) believe that "political correctness is a serious problem in our country, making it hard for people to say what they really think."[37] This view holds across the board, though an even greater percentage of those with lower educational attainment and people of conservative religious faith tend to share this opinion.

If people aren't saying what is really on their mind, then there is a basic problem of honesty in communication. This is a serious problem at any time, of course, but it is especially problematic in public discourse. Many see this as one of the fundamental problems in our democracy. *The Economist*, for example, has described our moment and our political discourse as a "post-truth world," a world in which feelings trump facts more freely and

---

and Schneider report the results of a 1980 Roper survey in which 71 percent of respondents believed that many top business executives engage in bribes and payoffs in return for political favors.

37 This suggests an increase in concern over political correctness since 2014, when a Rasmussen Reports poll (http://www.rasmussenreports.com/public_content/politics/general_politics/june_2014/61_think_america_is_too_politically_correct) found that 61 percent of respondents felt that America had become too politically correct.

effortlessly than ever before. Today, it would seem, public figures — politicians most prominently — are expedient with truth. Both of the candidates in the 2016 general election had challenges on this front.

The problem is reflected in the *2016 Survey of American Political Culture*. Two-thirds of the American public (67%) have little to *no confidence at all* "in the people who run our government to tell the truth to the public." As Machiavelli observed, the problem of truth may be endemic to politics. But even if it isn't, the perception that politicians play fast and loose with the truth has been with us for a while. In 1996, sixty-one percent of the American public held this same conviction. That may not seem like a significant change over two decades, but the difference is that these views have, once again, hardened a bit: In 1996, one-fourth (25%) held the most extreme view that they had "no confidence at all" that our political leadership tells the truth; Twenty years later, almost one-third (31%) feel this way.[38]

The problem of truth is not confined to politicians. It also extends to the one institution whose civic purpose is to convey accurate information to the public: the media. Three out of four Americans (74%) agree that "you can't believe much of what you hear from the mainstream media."[39] While popular trust in the media "to report the news fully, accurately and fairly" has been slowly declining for many years,[40] a clear majority now doubt the media's veracity. Given the importance of good journalism — and the information it provides to an electorate and a vital democracy — this is an extraordinary development. The media, many now believe, are not trusted to convey the basic information needed for substantive political engagement.

---

38 Trust in the government to tell the truth was higher in 2003 than in 1996 or today; the 2003 *Difference and Democracy* survey found that only 16 percent of respondents had no confidence at all in the people who run the government to tell the truth to the public, with 24 percent expressing only a little confidence. The elevated level of trust in 2003 may be linked to the fact that the terrorist attacks of September 11, 2001, had occurred only two years prior. In their aftermath, as Carl Bowman writes in his article, "The Evidence for Empire" (*The Hedgehog Review*, Spring 2003), "Whether the subject is one of flying the American flag or support for the President, Americans are clearly enjoying a celebration of nation not witnessed since the end of World War II."

39 The 1990 *Life Choices* survey found less cynicism regarding the media. While only 10 percent of respondents felt that the mass media were "very fair" in "their reporting public issues and events," fully 60 percent described the media as "fair."

40 See http://www.gallup.com/poll/185927/americans-trust-media-remains-historical-low.aspx.

Figure 4: Opinions of Media

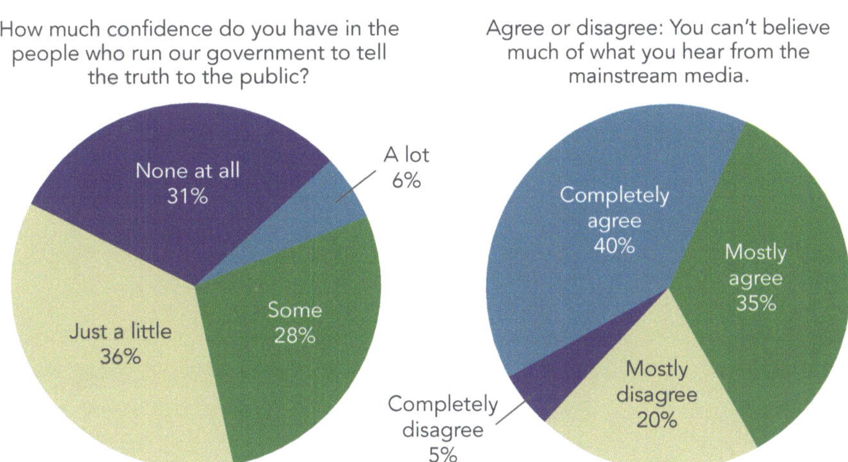

The Social Contract

The political distrust Americans have of each other doesn't run quite as deep as it does for the government, but it is extensive all the same. Half of the respondents (53%) had just a little or no confidence "in the wisdom of the American people when it comes to electing their national leaders."[41] This distrust is rooted in the low opinion they have of their neighbors' slapdash approach to political affairs. Eighty-six percent of all respondents agreed that "most Americans vote without really thinking through the issues."

41 A Pew report (http://www.people-press.org/files/2015/11/11-23-2015-Governance-release.pdf) compared responses to a similar question from 1964, 1997, 2007, and 2015. In 1964, 77 percent of respondents had either a "very great deal" or a "good deal" of trust and confidence "in the wisdom of the American people when it comes to making political decisions." Two-thirds (64%) were similarly confident in 1997, and 57 percent were as confident as recently as 2007. But in 2015, only 35 percent of respondents were confident in the wisdom of their fellow citizens.

Nevertheless, Americans generally (71%) want to believe — at least for themselves — that "if you follow the rules and behave responsibly, you can pretty much expect life will turn out well." Yet they also recognize that this is more difficult than it used to be. Three out of five respondents (59%) agree that "America used to be a place where you could get ahead by working hard, but this is no longer true."[42] Indeed, 41 percent believe that "hard work and determination are no guarantee of success for most Americans."[43]

Personal Alienation

Disaffection from the governing institutions of a social order can be seen as fairly abstract and the influences of the large-scale organizations as powerful, but still remote from everyday life. Yet Americans experience these concerns very personally. We have seen how strong majorities of Americans believe that politicians and leaders in business, the media, education and technology don't care about ordinary people like them; that these leaders and the institutions they represent serve primarily themselves, not average people or the common good. We also know that these tendencies in public opinion are now broadly if not deeply etched into American self-understanding. It is not surprising that a significant minority — nearly four out of ten Americans (38%) — agree that "these days, I feel like a stranger in my own country."

---

42 This maps onto other surveys. In early 2016, an NBC/*Esquire* poll (http://www.esquire.com/news-politics/a40693/american-rage-nbc-survey) found that 52 percent of the American public believe the idea of the American dream, "that if you work hard, you'll get ahead," once was true, but isn't anymore.

43 This finding echoes a 2015 CBS News/*New York Times* poll (http://www.cbsnews.com/news/poll-who-can-get-ahead-in-the-u-s/) in which only 35 percent of respondents agreed that "anyone has a fair chance" to get ahead in today's economy.

The Most Common Complaints

To give a sense of the high levels of consensus about the pathologies of American political culture, consider a list of complaints and criticisms along with the percentage of respondents agreeing.

Objection	Percent in Agreement
Most politicians are more interested in winning elections than in doing what is right.	90
Political events these days seem more like theater or entertainment than like something to be taken seriously.	88
Most Americans vote without really thinking through the issues.	86
Wall Street and big businesses in our country often profit at the expense of ordinary Americans.	84
You can't believe much of what you hear from the mainstream media.	75
Most elected officials don't care what people like me think.	74
Political correctness is a serious problem in our country, making it hard for people to say what they really think.	73
Our economic system is rigged in favor of the wealthiest Americans.	73
We need a President who will completely change the direction of this country.	72
Our system of government is good, but the people running it are incompetent.	71
People like me don't have any say about what the government does.	63

What Americans really need is a new political party because the current two-party system isn't working.	63
The leaders in American corporations, media, universities, and technology care little about the lives of most Americans.	62
The most educated and successful people in America are more interested in serving themselves than in serving the common good.	62
America used to be a place where you could get ahead by working hard, but this is no longer true.	59
The best government is the one which governs the least.	59
The American way of life is rapidly disappearing.	58
These days, the government in Washington threatens the freedom of ordinary Americans.	56
The United States has been too weak in dealing with other nations.	54
Our founding fathers were part of a racist and sexist culture that gave important roles to white men while harming minorities and women.	52
The police and law enforcement unfairly target racial and ethnic minorities.	45
People of other races can't really understand how my race sees things.	45
These days I feel like a stranger in my own country.	38
Most Americans who live in poverty are there because of their own bad choices and habits.	37

The types of complaint range widely, but it is especially remarkable how broadly they are shared. Discontent has become a familiar feature of American political culture, and it shows no signs of diminishing.

How Radical a Change?

Given the extent of disaffection, it is not surprising that Americans want change. Only about one in ten (9%) believe that the American "system of government is good and needs very little change." Against this, about one-third (33%) believe that the American "system of government is fine, but the people running it need to be changed." Nearly half (46%) want to go further, believing that "major changes are needed in both the system and the people running it." Beyond this, one out of eight Americans (12%) take the most radical position that "the system of government itself is broken and needs to be replaced with something completely different."

Figure 5: Need for Change

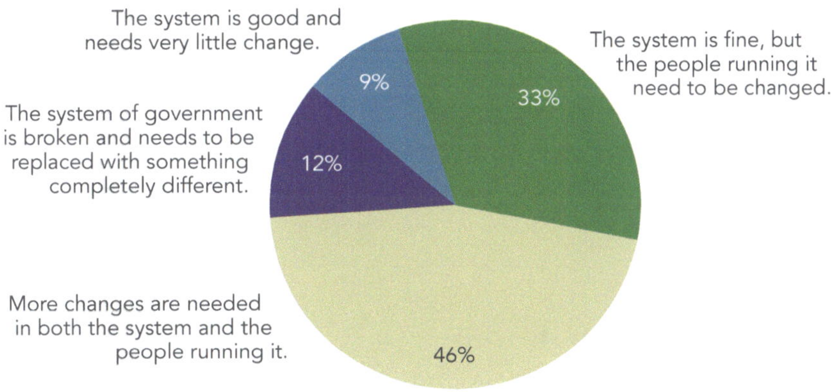

Reinforcing this demand for change is the fact that more than seven in ten Americans (72%) agree that we need "a President who will completely change the direction of this country;" 40 percent "completely agree." Do Americans want a change so radical as to undercut the system of checks and balances? We asked, "If we had a President you really believed in and trusted, would you want the President's actions to be limited by Congress and the Courts, as they are now, or would you want the President authorized to enact his or her agenda even if Congress did not support it?" Four out of five Americans (81%) said that they would want to retain the system of checks and balances, but one in five (19%) said that the president "should be authorized to act without Congressional support."

How Sustainable?

For many decades now, political theorists — and social scientists more generally — have worried about what seems to be a growing crisis of legitimacy of the governing authorities and institutions of Western democracies, including those of the United States. The historical evidence for such a legitimation crisis is extensive, and the *2016 Survey of American Political Culture* points to its reality in this particular moment. Some levels of popular discontent with government are inevitable in a democracy. It is, after all, difficult to please everyone. At the same time, it is important to note that the levels of discontent have grown and, in places, hardened.

While the majority of respondents want change, and some even want drastic change, public opinion doesn't suggest that Americans overall want to burn their system down. Far from it — or at least as of now. But even if this is the case, can such levels of discontent and disaffection safely subsist within the system without arriving at a tipping point that triggers outright popular and populist rejection of the system? Is this what we witnessed in the remarkable rise of Donald Trump? Are people so discontented that they are looking for any "spectacular" alternative as long as it is clearly an alternative? [44]

There is more to learn from the survey.

---

44 Roger Cohen suggests as much in "We Need Somebody Spectacular: Views From Trump Country," where he makes the case that Appalachian voters know perfectly well that Trump is dangerous, but they're willing to take the risk. *The New York Times*. September 9, 2016. Available at http://www.nytimes.com/2016/09/11/opinion/sunday/we-need-somebody-spectacular-views-from-trump-country.html?_r=0. Accessed October 1, 2016.

II

THE CONTOURS OF DISAFFECTION

The disaffection at the heart of the legitimation crisis in American public life is not one-dimensional, but multifactorial. It is not unlike the distinction made in social theory among class, status and power. Though these may be correlated as structures of inequality, they are not the same thing; they need to be distinguished. The same is true of disaffection: It is important to tease out separate factors to clarify the changing dynamics underwriting democratic practice in America. By combining and correlating specific questions from the survey, one can not only isolate those factors from each other, but derive summary indicators that will help give a better sense of the uneven landscape of disaffection.

The Dimensions of Disaffection

Distrust, Cynicism, and Alienation

For the purposes of this inquiry, *distrust* toward government is understood through the relative degrees of trust or confidence that the government can solve problems and tell the truth, and that what it communicates through the media is believable; that it won't intrude upon the freedoms that Americans enjoy; and that its leaders are competent to do their jobs.[45] *Cynicism* toward

---

45 The questions constituting the "distrust" index were: "When the government in Washington decides to solve a problem, how much confidence do you have that the problem will actually be solved?"; "How much confidence do you have in the people who run our government to tell the truth to the public?"; "Our system of government is good, but the people running it are incompetent."; "These days, the government in Washington threatens the freedom of ordinary Americans."; and "You can't believe much of what you hear from the mainstream media." The

leaders is defined by opinions about whether leaders and other elites are more interested in serving themselves than the common good, are more interested in keeping power than doing what is right, and are indifferent toward the lives and thoughts of ordinary people.[46] Finally, *alienation* is, in effect, a personal sense of estrangement from the world around you. This includes a sense of having little or no agency in the ordering of the world. It is reflected in the view that "the American way of life is rapidly disappearing," that "America used to be a place where you could get ahead by working hard, but this is no longer true," and that compared to 25 years ago, you are worse off.[47]

statement about the media is, in our view, as much about the veracity of what the public hears about the government as it is about the media as a purveyor of information. When the media item is omitted, the patterns remain the same, but the Cronbach's alpha for the index drops from .774 to .754.

46 The questions constituting this index are: "The most educated and successful people in America are more interested in serving themselves than in serving the common good," "Most politicians are more interested in winning elections than in doing what is right," "The leaders in American corporations, media, universities and technology care little about the lives of most Americans," and "Most elected officials don't care what people like me think." Alpha for this index is .671, which is relatively high for an index comprised of only four ordinal measures.

47 The questions constituting the alienation index are: "The American way of life is rapidly disappearing," "America used to be a place where you could get ahead by working hard, but this is no longer true," "These days I feel like a stranger in my own country," "People like me don't have any say about what the government does," and "Would you say people like you are doing much better, better, about the same, worse or much worse than twenty-five years ago?" Alpha for the index is .746. For all three indices — distrust, cynicism and alienation — EM estimation of individual item scores was used to replace missing data and principal components analysis was used to assign item weights.

Figure 6: Dimensions of Disaffection[48]

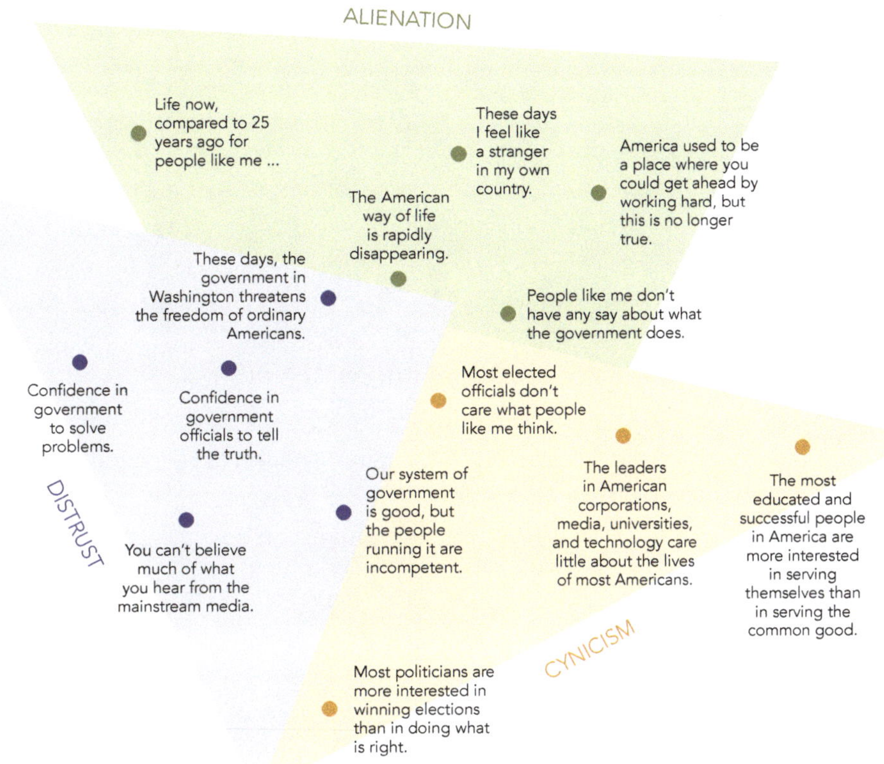

As we've seen, all of these dimensions of disaffection are fairly widely distributed across the population, but the full complexity of the story is revealed only by examining the patterns of interaction among the different categories of disaffection. The first thing to note is that disaffection can be focused privately or publicly, toward the personal or the institutional. Alienation — with its sense of becoming marginalized, of losing, of working without reaping, of not being seen or heard, and of things spiraling downward — is the private face of disaffection, while cynicism toward leaders, experts, officials and those in positions of power (as well as distrust of public institutions) constitute the dual public face of disaffection. The

---

48 Distances between the statements of disaffection in this figure were assigned using a Multidimensional Scaling of Tau measures of association between the individual items.

interplay between the personal and the institutional is difficult to discern. What follows is our first attempt to interpret some of these dynamics.

The closer the statements in Figure 6, the greater the similarity in how Americans respond to them. A private statement that "People like me don't have any say," for instance, is closely tied to the more institutionally framed view that "Most elected officials don't care what people like me think." And the latter sense that officials don't care is related closely to views that they will lie to the public and that they are incompetent. It is important to recognize that the converse to these patterns is also true. Those who retain confidence in the media, for example, are also less inclined to say government officials are incompetent or that they fail to tell the truth. They are also among those most likely to still believe that government can really solve problems when it sets its mind to. And the distance between these statements on the left and one on the far right-hand side of the chart about "the most educated and successful people in America" reflects the fact that confidence in government ebbs and flows somewhat independently of confidence in the highly educated and the wealthy; they don't necessarily rise and fall together.

It is also informative to consider how the dimensions of disaffection vary across particular groups in society. *Distrust toward the government*, for example, does not differ significantly for different income groups in America. It does, however, differ by their age, gender, race and residence. Distrust is one-and-a-half times more likely to be very high among Baby Boomers, for example, than Millennials, higher among men than women, and higher among those who live in less populated areas than in urban areas of the country. Distrust is twice as likely to be very high among whites as among Hispanics or African-Americans, and almost as much difference in levels of trust exists between religious conservatives, whether Protestant or Catholic, and their more moderate and progressive counterparts.[49]

---

49 Quartile-cut versions of the distrust, cynicism, and alienation indices were utilized for these comparisons. For narrative purposes, respondents who scored in the highest quartile — among the highest twenty-five percent — are considered "very high," and the second quartile, simply "high." Together, these two groups constitute the half of respondents that are highest on each index. The terms "low" and "very low" are employed similarly to describe the bottom two quartiles, which together encompass those who score in the lower half on each index.

In the case of *cynicism toward elites*, a person's generation, region of the country and ethnicity offer little clue about their cynicism. The same generally goes for gender, even though women are slightly less cynical about experts, leaders and elected officials than are men. Similarly, the population density where one lives is only loosely connected to cynicism — those who live in rural areas tend to be slightly more cynical toward elites. The key elements tied to cynicism are income and education, especially the latter. Here, cynicism is twice as likely to be very high among those earning less than $25,000 per year than among those earning $250,000 or more per year. In the case of education, cynicism is three-and-a-half times more likely to be very high for those who have a high school diploma or less than for those who have undertaken post-graduate studies.

Finally, personal *alienation*, which includes the sense of being powerless and culturally marginalized, reveals no significant gender or racial differences. Evangelicals, however, are more alienated than non-Evangelical Protestants with the latter nearly twice as likely to score low on alienation. The contrast between conservative Catholics and progressive Catholics is equally pronounced. Interestingly, the religious group that is most likely to score low on personal alienation is the one that claims no religious affiliation at all — the "nones." Generation too is an important axis of difference on alienation, with baby boomers one-and-a-half times more likely to be highly alienated, as we have defined it here, than Millennials. Even more significant is your education, income and the population density of your neighborhood: Alienation rates are twice as likely to be very high in the most rural areas as in the denser cities; three-and-a-half times more likely if you have only a high school diploma than a graduate degree; and four times more likely if you are in the lowest income bracket than if you belong in the highest income bracket. As with distrust of political institutions and cynicism about America's "experts" and leaders, personal alienation is more closely tied to education and income than to other measures of social location.

The Deepest Disaffection

A certain amount of disaffection is found across all categories: men and women; young and old; white, black and Hispanic; rich and poor; and so on. And yet there is also no question that the patterns we are seeing confirm what we know both anecdotally and from other survey work: that there is a predictable unevenness — some are more completely, even stridently, disaffected than others.

When one considers all dimensions of disaffection together and looks to their cumulative impact, one sees the greatest intensity of total disaffection in a population that tends to be more *male* than female,[50] disproportionately represented among *Baby Boomers*,[51] and among those who reside in the *lowest density* parts of the country, though not in any particular region of the country.[52] It is notable that minorities are under-represented at very high levels of disaffection (only 31% of African-Americans and 35% of Hispanics are among the top 40% of disaffected overall) yet nearly half of all whites are found among the highest groups of disaffected. Less surprising is the fact that the most disaffected are disproportionately *poor*: 53 percent of those who make less than $50,000 per year have very high disaffection compared to 14 percent of persons making over $100,000 per year.[53] The pattern intensifies further with education: Most of the disaffected are *poorly educated*. Among the most disaffected, 84 percent don't have a college degree, compared to 16 percent who do.[54] Religious faith seems to be less determinative than additive. The more *conservative* you are in your faith, the more likely you will have higher levels of disaffection.

The Demand for Change

Among those who are most disaffected — the most distrustful, cynical, and alienated — roughly three out of four (72%) want major changes: one-fourth (24%) believe that "the system of government itself is broken and needs to be replaced with something completely different"; one-half (48%) believe that major

---

50 About half (47%) of all who are in the highest two levels of disaffection are men compared to 39 percent who are women.

51 In very high levels of disaffection, respondents are one-and-a-half times more likely to be a Boomer than a Gen Xer or a Millennial.

52 About half (53%) of all who have a very high disaffection live in the lowest two levels of population density. If you live in the least populated rural areas, you are twice as likely to be in the highest category of disaffection.

53 Seen another way, half (48%) of all those who make less than $50,000 per year have very high disaffection compared to one-third (34%) of all those who make more than $100,000 per year.

54 Again, seen differently, one out of two people who have some college or only a high school diploma or less (50%) have very high disaffection, compared to one out of four who have a post-graduate degree.

changes are needed in both the system and the people running it. Likewise, 98 percent of the most totally disaffected agree that "we need a President who will completely change the direction of this country."

The Least Disaffected

As noted, disaffection is inarguably found everywhere in the population, but unevenly. Those who are most disaffected tend to have a certain profile, but this is also true of those who are less disaffected.

American Dreamers: African-Americans and Hispanics

African-Americans and Hispanics love their country and think highly of it as much as white Americans. Nearly half (47%) of all blacks and Latinos (42%) believe that America "is the greatest country in the world, better than all other countries" and nearly as many (45% and 49% respectively) see America as "a great country, but so are certain other countries." Eight of ten (80% of blacks and 82% of Latinos) also agree that "America is an exceptional nation with a special responsibility to lead the world." The vast majority (80% African-American, 78% Hispanic) agree that they are "proud to live under our American system of government." Even so, their patriotism has a distinctly different tone than that of white Americans. Whites are nearly twice as likely as blacks and Hispanics to say they are "very patriotic," while blacks and Hispanics prefer the more subdued "moderately patriotic" option.[55]

If anything, both blacks and Hispanics exude greater confidence in the United States government than whites. This is particularly notable in the small numbers of Hispanics (22%) and blacks (12%) who have "no confidence at all" in the ability of government to solve problems and in the people who run our government to tell the truth to the public (Hispanics: 22%; blacks: 19%; and whites: 36%). In general, whites are twice as likely as blacks and Hispanics to be very distrustful of the government on a variety of measures. Their disparate levels of trust are mirrored in disparate philosophies of government — a majority of whites believe government is doing too many things that are better left to private entities and individuals, while two-thirds

---

55 Two-thirds of whites say they are "very patriotic" compared to 35% of Hispanics and 35% of blacks.

of Hispanics (65%) and blacks (69%) believe government should actually be doing *more* to improve the lives of ordinary Americans.

That the trust of minorities extends to the current president is not surprising given his own minority status, but the extent of that difference — 94 percent of blacks view Obama favorably as do 78 percent of Latinos, compared to 44 percent of whites — is striking. These respective levels of support are reflected in black and Latino levels of opposition to changing immigration policies, building a wall between the U.S. and Mexico, repealing the Affordable Care Act and banning U.S. entry to all Muslims. Minorities generally oppose all of these changes in policy. Their disproportionate residence in densely populated urban centers, their tendency to identify as Democrats and Independents rather than Republicans, and perhaps their experiences of violence, threats of violence, and suspicions of violence in their own communities may all inform their distinctive view of guns in public spaces. More than four out of five African-Americans (83%) and more than three out of five Hispanics (62%) say it would make our nation a more dangerous place if more Americans legally carried weapons in public. Only a minority of whites (43%) say the same.

Figure 7: Guns in Public Places

If more Americans legally carried weapons in public,
do you think it would make our nation ... ?

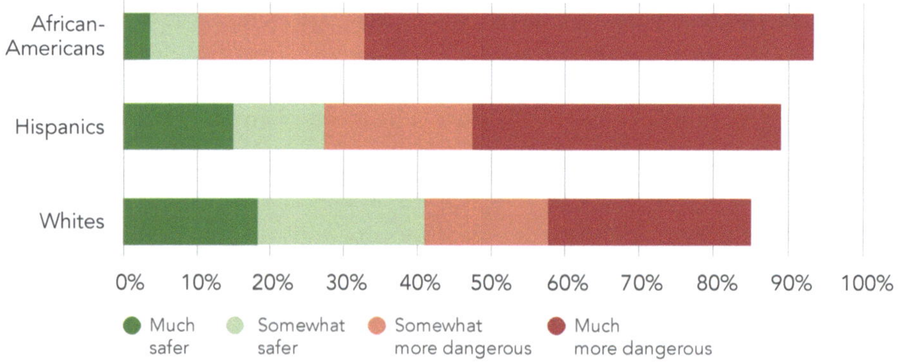

The high confidence levels of minorities also extend beyond government to broader perceptions of the state of the nation. Seven out of ten blacks (70%) and Hispanics (72%), for example, believe the United States is not a nation in decline, but is instead holding steady or improving; only a minority of whites (43%) say the same.

Figure 8: State of the Nation

Is the United States declining, holding steady, or improving?

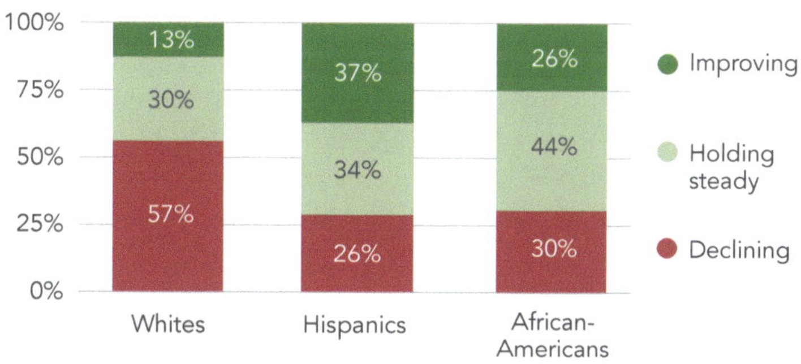

This disparity parallels differences in minority views of what has happened to "people like you" during the past twenty-five years. Only one in five African-Americans (19%) and Hispanics (20%) say they are worse off, compared to nearly half of whites (43%) who say they have it worse. Hispanics in particular say the "quality of life for their racial or ethnic group in the U.S." has improved in recent years — they are three times more likely to say this than are whites.

These positive impressions of the United States — what it stands for and how it functions — are especially notable in light of perceptions of history and social circumstances. Eight out of ten (81%) blacks and six out of ten (60%) Latinos agree that "our founding fathers were part of a racist and sexist culture that gave important roles to white men while harming minorities and women;" only a minority of whites (45%) subscribe to this historical narrative. Minority perceptions of police and law enforcement are even more distinct from those of whites. Sizable majorities of blacks (83%) and Hispanics (63%) say "the police and law enforcement unfairly target racial and ethnic minorities" compared to only a third (33%) of white Americans. The same pattern is reflected in the greater sense among minorities that "people of other races can't really understand how my race sees things." Three-fourths (74%) of all blacks agree with that statement compared to just over half (55%) of all Latinos and only one-third (36%) of all whites.

The resilience of African-American and Hispanic faith in government and nation is also striking in light of their personal social circumstances. Only 14 percent of Hispanics and 21 percent of African-Americans (by our survey estimates) have a college degree, compared to 35 percent of whites. And substantial majorities of both blacks (62%) and Latinos (72%) get by on family incomes of less than $50,000 a year compared to only a minority of whites (37%). Given their material circumstances, it is not surprising that 62 percent of all African-Americans and 56 percent of all Hispanics describe their family's current financial situation as "only fair" or "poor" compared to 45 percent of all whites. Though not dramatic, a larger number of blacks (45%) and Hispanics (40%) do agree that "these days I feel like a stranger in my own country" compared to 36 percent of all whites. African-Americans are particularly inclined to say the economic system is rigged in favor of the wealthiest Americans — half of them (48%) "completely agree" this is how the economy operates, compared to less than thirty percent of Hispanics (28%) and whites (29%). Adding those who "mostly agree," more than 70 percent of all three groups say the economy is rigged.

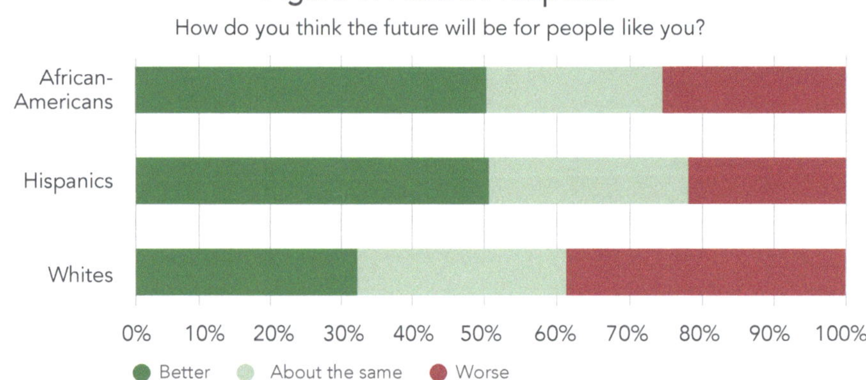

Figure 9: Future Prospects

How do you think the future will be for people like you?

In spite of perceptions of historical and contemporary injustice, and even in the face of challenging social circumstances, Hispanics and African-Americans remain hopeful and faithful. Half (49 percent of Hispanics and 48 percent of blacks) believe the future for people like themselves will be better in twenty-five years. Another quarter believe it will be about the same, and only a quarter think it will be worse (compared to 40 percent of whites who think things will be worse). Hispanics have an especially strong conviction that "if you follow the rules and behave responsibly, you can pretty much expect life will turn out well"; 78 percent agree with that statement. A majority of African-Americans

(58%) agree with this as well, though not to the same degree.[56] A substantial majority of Hispanics (67%) also believe Americans can "make it if they're willing to work hard," yet only a minority of blacks (47%) hold this opinion. While African-American faith in the long-term rewards of hard work may be weaker than for more recent immigrants, their religious faith remains strong. African-Americans report a distinctively active prayer life — two-thirds say they pray daily — and a sense that people who are not religious do not share their beliefs and values (60%).

It is hardly surprising that on many questions in the survey, we find as pervasive disaffection in minority communities as we have in the white population. Indeed, minority levels of cynicism toward leaders and experts, and their personal alienation and feelings of lack of agency, are comparable to the levels in the white community. Yet against all odds and difficulties, the African-American and Hispanic communities tend to see a brighter future for themselves. They continue to pursue the American Dream and perhaps for this reason — at least insofar as confidence in government and in their own situation is concerned — they are less disaffected. And this in spite of their lower incomes, lower levels of education and "their experiences as minorities in American society."

The Wealthy and Well-Educated

The other group that is less disaffected is elites, those who are disproportionately well-educated and wealthy. Among the wealthiest, 92 percent of those making over $250,000 and 81 percent of those making between $100,000 and $250,000 describe their financial situation as excellent or good (and well they should!). Seventy-one percent of those with post-graduate degrees describe their financial circumstances the same way. Two-thirds of the biggest income earners also acknowledge that they are doing much better or better than 25 years ago compared to 37 percent of those in the lowest income bracket. These are individuals who are comfortably situated in life, and they know it.

Perhaps it is for this reason that, as a group, they tend to have greater agency and thus less alienation, less cynicism, and greater trust in government

---

56 On this point, 71 percent of whites hold this view.

compared to those who have less. The findings are consistent. About one-third (30%) of all who are making over $250,000 per year have a very high trust in government, compared to 21 percent of the poorest in this category. This holds for those who have a post-graduate degree — 34 percent have a very high level of trust, compared to 20 percent with a high school diploma or less. The same is true for patterns of cynicism: 42 percent of the wealthiest Americans have a very high trust in leaders compared to 17 percent of the poorest. Thirty-five percent of those with very high levels of educational attainment have high levels of belief in their leaders compared to 17 percent of the most poorly educated. Finally, and not surprisingly, the wealthiest have the greatest sense of agency: One in four (39%) of the wealthiest have very low alienation compared to 14 percent of the poorest. Likewise, with the best educated: 35 percent have a very low alienation compared to 16 percent of the most poorly educated.

It is entirely plausible that their general lack of cynicism, distrust, and alienation (as compared to others) could be a reflection of their circumstances. It is entirely plausible that for these reasons, as well, the wealthiest are the most likely to say that "the system is good and needs very little change" and are the least likely to say that "the system of government itself is broken and needs to be replaced with something completely different." Half (51%) of all those with postgraduate degrees also disagree that "we need a President who will completely change the direction of this country."

III

THE NEW CULTURE WARS

For most of the twentieth century, the axis of tension and conflict defining Right and Left in American politics and beyond was rooted in political economy. It was a division between wealth and poverty, and so many of the specific policy arguments — whether about fair labor practices, public housing, aid to families with dependent children, education, and the like — were ultimately tensions centered on the concentration or redistribution of wealth.

It is not as if those conflicts disappeared, but in the 1970s, they began to recede as a new axis of tension and conflict emerged, one that was fundamentally cultural in nature. At the root of this new conflict were competing understandings of the good and how the good is grounded and legitimated. These understandings were reflected in competing moral visions of collective life and the discourse sustaining those visions.

The historical significance of the "culture war" was seen in the ways in which this new axis cut across age-old divisions between Protestants and Catholics and Jews. The orthodox traditions in these faiths had come to have much more in common with one another than they do with progressives in their own faith tradition and vice versa. The polarity of *this* axis seemed to better account for variation of opinions and positions on a wide range of popular domestic disputes: abortion, sexuality, the changing role of women and the changing nature of the family, church-state issues, funding for the arts and so on, than did traditional axes such as religious affiliation, gender, socio-economic standing and race/ethnicity. These disputes not only divided America, but other parts of both the developing and developed world.[57]

---

57 Peter L. Berger (ed.), *Die Grenzen der Gemeinschaft*, Verlag Bertelsmann/Club of Rome, 1997.

In turn, it was around the new polarities of *these* controversies — over what became known as "moral issues" — that a far-reaching struggle for national identity took place.

It is important to stress that the cultural conflict that defined so much of American politics for nearly four decades was always one taking place *within* the middle class. Yes, there were class elements to this conflict, but they were mainly the differences between the lower-middle and upper-middle classes.

In the intervening years, the intra-class tensions have intensified and, in our view, transformed into what is best considered two very different social locations within the middle class, *yet with significantly different class cultures*.[58] These cultures are marked not only by different values, beliefs and sensibilities, but also by strikingly different life chances. This is the heart of the new culture war.

The backdrop for this is a significant change within the *objective* conditions of middle class life during the past half century; a change that was amplified and highlighted in public consciousness by the "Great Recession." Since 2008, awareness of a cleavage between the highly educated, professional upper-middle class on the one hand, and the less well-educated, non-professional middle, low-middle and working class on the other, has deepened and hardened. The former were surprised and even shaken by the economic contraction, but were not broadly traumatized by its harsh effects, while the latter felt much of the recession, if not its full impact.

Even as a new cultural conflict has overshadowed the old one, it isn't as though the conflict of the previous four decades disappeared — it hasn't. But it has been transformed, mainly by the reemergence of tensions rooted in political economy. These new class cleavages are at the heart of the new social dynamics that account for much of the undercurrent of American political culture. A comparison among these classes brings into relief the disparity of perceptions about their country, their experience within it and, ultimately, their political orientation.

---

58 "Middle class" here is to be understood broadly. These class cultures are attached to very real differences in educational achievement and material circumstances, which could alternatively be viewed as different class locations.

Complexity and Polarity in Public Opinion

It is essential to note that the culture war of the past 40 years was primarily a conflict that took shape within public discourse as it was mediated by powerful institutions — among them, political parties, special interest groups, philanthropies and professional associations — and given articulation by its leaders. In *this* way, cultural conflict took shape as a fairly sharp binary between conservatives and progressives.

In actual public opinion, however, the attitudes of ordinary Americans never divided so neatly. Quite the opposite, in fact, as survey after survey documented great complexity in their attitudes and opinions.[59] But with all of that acknowledged, there was also the inescapable fact that there were extremes in public opinion that represented the rank and file of citizens united around the opposing positions in public discourse.[60] These constituted somewhere between 10 to 15 percent of the population at each end of the ideological spectrum.

In the 2016 Survey of American Political Culture we find similar dynamics at play, but we begin with a simple distinction.

The Evolving Cultural Divide

In a post-industrial, global and knowledge-based economy, facility with symbolic skills and the educational credentials to prove it are, as a rule, foundational to success in the middle class. They open the door to careers,

---

59 See, for example, an extensive study of public opinion on the politics of abortion in "The Anatomy of Ambivalence," by J. D. Hunter and Carl Bowman, (Chapter 5) in J. D. Hunter, *Before the Shooting Begins: Searching for Democracy in America's Culture Wars.* New York: Free Press, 1994.

60 See Carl Desportes Bowman, "The Myth of a Non-Polarized America." *The Hedgehog Review.* Fall 2010. Available at http://www.iasc-culture.org/THR/THR_article_2010_Fall_Bowman.php. Accessed October 3, 2016.

upward mobility and salaries that are otherwise, generally, beyond reach. It isn't surprising, then, that a key line of distinction emerges in this survey between the Credentialed and the Non-Credentialed.[61]

The Credentialed are those who have achieved a four-year college degree. They are comparably wealthy: Over four out of ten (45%) have family incomes of more than $100,000 per year compared to 25 percent of the total sample. Moreover, they are aware of their good fortune: 72 percent describe their current financial situation as "good" or "excellent." As a group, they are fairly evenly spread among the generations following the general distribution. They also range across the country, and they tend to reside in the most demographically dense population areas. Religiously, they are diverse — Christian, Jewish and secularist — though they tend to be moderate to liberal in their orientation.

The Non-Credentialed are those with at best some college education, but often only a high school diploma or less. For lack of a college credential, they tend to be at a distinct educational and economic disadvantage. Almost three out of four (72%) have family incomes of less than $75,000 per year. Unlike the Credentialed, most of the Non-Credentialed (55%) describe their family's financial circumstances as "only fair" or "poor," and most imagine a future for themselves that is much the same as it is now (28%) or worse (29%). They, too, are spread across the country, though slightly more highly represented in the Midwest and, not surprisingly, disproportionately represented in the less densely populated regions of the country. Religiously, they also are diverse and, while more conservative than the Credentialed, they are still, overall, fairly moderate in their religious views.

---

61 Our description and analysis here of the Credentialed and the Non-Credentialed focuses specifically upon the cleavage in class cultures among white Americans. Where political culture is concerned, African-Americans and Hispanics display patterns that are unique to their own histories and experiences as minority groups in America. Because of their uniqueness, we considered them separately in the preceding section, just as we consider the cultural cleavage between Credentialed and Non-Credentialed whites in this section. The extent to which the cultural cleavages of the "new culture war" pertain to black and Latino communities remains to be investigated, but our preliminary analysis of the data suggests that in 2016, the cleavage is largely one dividing white America. See Robert D. Putnam, *Our Kids: The American Dream in Crisis*; J. D. Vance, *Hillbilly Elegy: A Memoir of a Family and Culture in Crisis*; Arlie Russell Hochschild, *Strangers in the Own Land: Anger and Mourning on the American Right*; and Charles Murray, *Coming Apart: The State of White America, 1960-2010* for additional insights into the cultural and economic rift among white Americans.

This line of division has important consequences for how Americans understand political culture and politics itself. Consider, for example, the issue of disaffection. The Non-Credentialed are one-and-a-half times more likely than the Credentialed to have very high mistrust; nearly three times more likely to be highly cynical; and over twice as likely to express very high alienation. On our aggregate disaffection measure that bridges distrust, cynicism and alienation, the Non-Credentialed are three times more likely to have very high total disaffection than the Credentialed.

This fault line also plays out in different tendencies in worldview and public policy. For example, the Non-Credentialed (58%) are a bit more inclined than the Credentialed (49%) to think that "the government is doing too many things that are better left to businesses, civic groups and individuals," whereas the Credentialed (51%) tend to think that the government should do more to improve the lives of ordinary Americans.

To take another example, a strong majority (81%) of the Credentialed take the view that "immigrants strengthen our country because of their hard work and talents" compared to just over half (58%) of the Non-Credentialed. This line of reasoning is reflected in views on immigration policy: 39 percent of the Credentialed are in favor of greatly reducing the number of immigrants entering the United States, compared to 61 percent of the Non-Credentialed. The same general pattern can be seen in the views toward "building a wall across the border between the U.S. and Mexico." Only 29 percent of Credentialed Americans take this view, compared to 49 percent of the Non-Credentialed.

The same pattern can be seen in political ideology, where 40 percent of the Credentialed think of themselves as somewhat or very liberal compared to 25 percent of the Non-Credentialed. It finally cashes out in voting behavior: 52 percent of the Non-Credentialed say they would vote for Trump; 32 percent say they would vote for Clinton; and 16 percent say they would vote for someone else (8%) or not at all (8%). The percentages are almost reversed for the Credentialed: half (49%) say they would vote for Clinton and only 36% would vote for Trump.

Belief as a Polarizing Factor: A Profile of the Disinherited and the Social Elite

Clearly, we see consistent patterns of difference of opinion rooted in education that, while hardly representing polarities, are pulling consistently in opposite directions. Education, then, is a clearly discernible crevasse in the political-cultural landscape. But how wide is this rift, and how deep does it go?

When we push the analysis further in two ways, it becomes apparent that even within the crevasse there are significant fault lines in American political culture. Our first analytic turn is to push the education factor out, beyond those who are merely credentialed to those who hold graduate degrees. By virtue of their educational credentials, they are the best positioned in the population to operate effectively in the global economy. The second analytical turn is to introduce the cultural factor central to the older culture war; namely, that of belief. Among the Non-Credentialed, we pull out those who are religiously conservative – in this case, mostly Evangelical Protestants and Conservative Catholics. Eight out of ten regard their faith as very important or the most important thing in their lives. They not only are at a disadvantage in the work of the global economy, but they also, as we will see, feel more and more like cultural outsiders because of their religious beliefs. Within the most highly educated sector of the population, where religious orthodoxy is rare, we hone in on those who are religiously moderate, liberal, and secular in their orientation. The former we call the *Disinherited*; the latter we call the *Social Elite*.

In short, the Disinherited have the same challenges as the broader group of Non-Credentialed to which they belong, but worse. Half (50%) live on less than $50,000 per year compared to 10 percent of the Social Elite. The majority of the Disinherited (58%) describe their family's current financial situation as "only fair" or "poor," with half (52%) seeing their prospects in the future as worse, 21 percent seeing their prospects as "much worse." Conversely, six out of ten (58%) of the Social Elite have family incomes that are $100,000 or over, compared to 13 percent of the Disinherited. The Social Elite are aware of their good fortune: 73 percent describe their current financial situation as "good" or "excellent" and an even stronger majority (79%) see their future as staying the same (36%) or getting better (43%).

Though the Disinherited and Social Elites are found across the generations, the former tend to be a bit older (the majority found primarily within the Baby Boom (40%) and Silent (22%) generations) where the majority of Social Elites tend to be found in the Baby Boom (30%) and Gen X (29%) generations. Social Elites also include a significant number (25%) of Millennials. These two groups sort themselves out in predictable regional distributions: Social Elites are concentrated on the coasts — New England, the Mid-Atlantic and the Far West — and they tend to reside in the most demographically dense population areas; the Disinherited are disproportionately found in the Midwest and Southeast in the least densely populated areas.

These lines of division — those pertaining to educational credentials and faith — are both familiar and new. Together they represent a rift that is at the heart of the new cultural conflict. This plays out on every front in ways that reveal deep fissures that are, in fact, fundamentally different world views.

In the analysis that follows, we add, as a point of reference, a third category: *the Disadvantaged*. They have the same educational profile as the Disinherited (high school diploma or less, or perhaps some college but no degree), but they are religiously moderate, liberal and secular.

A Deepening Disaffection

One of the ways in which these groups contrast is on the different dimensions of disaffection. The Disinherited are over seven times more likely, and the Disadvantaged over four times more likely, than Social Elites to have a very high distrust in government. Likewise, the Disinherited and the Disadvantaged are five times more likely than elites to be highly cynical of leadership. Not least, the Disinherited are over nine-and-a-half times more likely, and the Disadvantaged over six times more likely than Social Elites, to be highly alienated. Cumulatively, in terms of the total disaffection scale, the Disinherited are five times more likely, and the Disadvantaged are three-and-a-half times more likely, to score in the top levels of disaffection than are Social Elites. These are neither small nor subtle differences. They reflect an unfolding world that has left both the Disinherited and the Disadvantaged suspicious of governing institutions and contemptuous of their leadership, and this in the face of a pervasive sense of powerlessness to do anything about it politically or otherwise.

Cross-Cutting Lines of Solidarity and Difference

Another way in which we see these groups contrast is in how they perceive solidarity with some groups and differ from others. The legacy of racial conflict, ethnic tension, and religious prejudice has always been at war with the ideals of a vital center, and certainly those lines of difference haven't disappeared. So where are the lines of division now drawn?

In the *2016 Survey of American Political Culture*, we ask, "For the following groups, do you see their beliefs and values as being completely different, mostly different, mostly similar or completely the same as Americans like you?" Here is the mapping as it plays out in the general population:

Figure 10: Reported Cultural Distance

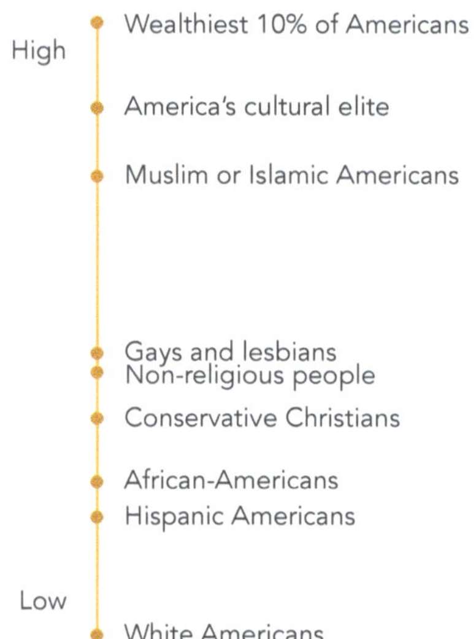

The greatest social distance is seen not along racial or ethnic lines, but along lines of class, with the wealthiest Americans and its cultural elite seen as furthest removed from the values and beliefs of the majority. The perception of difference from Muslim Americans is less than from the economic and cultural elite, but still quite strong. By comparison, the perceived cultural difference with African-Americans and Hispanics is relatively small.

This configuration alters dramatically when viewed across the new social divisions. The one thing that each of these groups share in common is the perception that the beliefs and values of the wealthiest Americans are dramatically different from their own. The sense of distance from the cultural elite is also strong, though predictably stronger among the Disinherited and the Disadvantaged than among the Social Elite. Another point of commonality is the sense of only a moderate distance from the values and beliefs of the African-American and Hispanic communities.[62]

Figure 11: Reported Cultural Distance

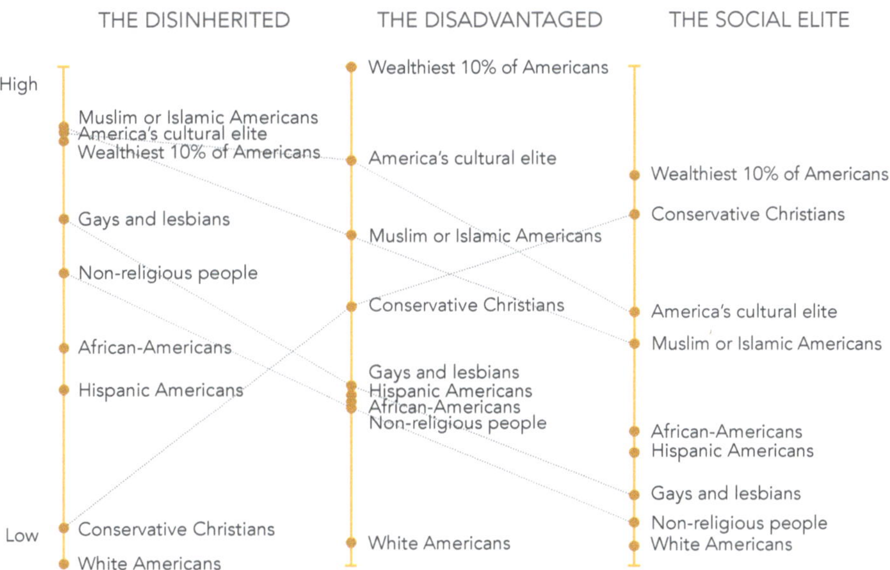

What stands out so starkly in this comparison are the discrepant perceptions of cultural distance from conservative Christians, gays and lesbians, non-religious people and Muslims. Where the Disinherited perceive very little cultural distance from conservative Christians, the Social Elite perceive the values and beliefs of conservative Christians as radically different.[63]

---

62 Keep in mind here that all three groups in this section — the Disinherited, Disadvantaged, and Social Elite — consist entirely of white respondents, since the new culture war being analyzed here is one within the white community.

63 This is largely a function of the fact that we have defined the Disinherited not only in terms of their lack of a four-year college credential, but also as those holding a religious conservative

The reverse is also true: Social Elites perceive only a minimal cultural distance from gays, lesbians and the non-religious, while the Disinherited see themselves as very different from all three. In all of these contrasts, the Disadvantaged hold middling positions, but there is nothing middling about the distance they perceive between their own beliefs and values and those of the wealthiest Americans.

Polarizing Visions for America

It is not surprising that these very different class-cultural positions predispose people toward vastly different visions of public policy. Consider first their different views of government. When asked to choose which statement comes closest to their view of the role of government, two-thirds (68%) of all Social Elites said, "government should do more to improve the lives of ordinary Americans" compared to 70 percent of the Disinherited who believe that "government is doing too many things that are better left to businesses, civic groups, and individuals." The Disadvantaged split roughly down the middle on these views.

Also consider immigration: 87 percent of all Social Elites take the view that "immigrants strengthen our country because of their hard work and talents." Two-thirds of the Disadvantaged (67%) take this view as well. This drops to only half (49%) among the Disinherited who hold this view, while the other half (51%) believe that "immigrants are a burden on our country who take jobs, housing, and health care." Not surprisingly, this division of opinion is reflected in views on immigration policy: 76 percent of the Disinherited are in favor of greatly reducing the number of immigrants entering the United States, compared to 51 percent of the Disadvantaged and less than a quarter (22 percent) of the Social Elite. The same general discrepancy can be seen in their views toward "building a wall across the border between the U.S. and Mexico." Two-thirds (66%) of the Disinherited favor building such a wall, compared to 32 percent of the Disadvantaged and only 9 percent of all Social Elites. It is not surprising that this pattern extends to attitudes toward the immigration of Muslims: 63 percent of all the Disinherited favor "banning

viewpoint. The latter is the only thing distinguishing them from the Disadvantaged who are similarly "non-credentialed."

entry to all Muslims until we better understand the terrorist threat to our country," compared to 36 percent of all of the Disadvantaged and just 14 percent of the Social Elite. These cultural discrepancies, associated with underlying differences in education and religiosity, go beyond the realm of simple contrast; they appear to reflect completely different cultural worlds.

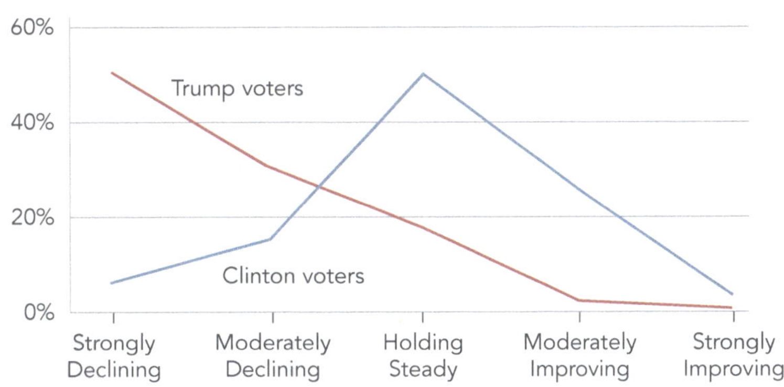

Figure 12: Divergent Perspectives

A San Andreas Fault runs through other policy perspectives as well. For example, four out of five (79%) of the Disinherited favor repealing the Affordable Care Act (or "Obamacare"), compared to 46 percent of the Disadvantaged and just a quarter (26%) of the Social Elite. And where the vast majority of the Social Elite (84%) and the Disadvantaged (83%) favor requiring all areas of the country to officially permit gay marriage, only one-third of the Disinherited (34%) favor this policy.

Finally, consider how the differences play out over guns. Roughly six in ten (61%) of the Disinherited believe that "if more Americans legally carried weapons in public" it would make the nation safer. This compares to one-third (33%) of the Disadvantaged and only 8 percent of the Social Elite.

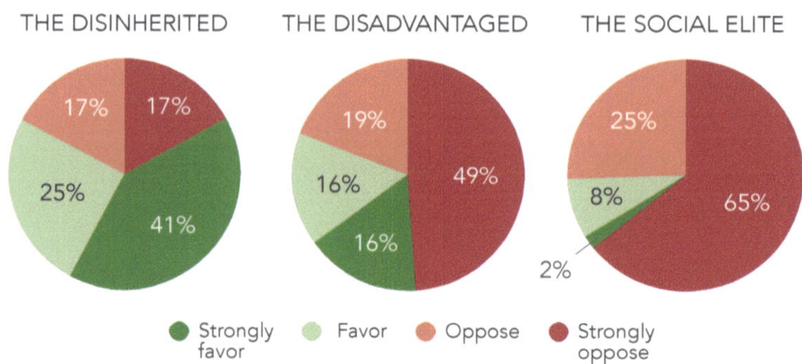

Figure 13: Immigration Viewed Within Social Groups

Do you favor or oppose building a wall across the border
between the U.S. and Mexico?

Sharpening Political Differences

At this point, there is little surprise in how these social and cultural
cleavages play out in political self-understanding. Two-thirds (69%) of all
the Disinherited view themselves as politically conservative, compared to
17 percent of the Disadvantaged and 9 percent of Social Elites. The mirror
opposite is true of the other side of the ideological divide: 59 percent of Social
Elites view themselves as politically liberal compared to 43 percent of the
Disadvantaged and just 8 percent of the Disinherited.

It follows that the majority of the Disinherited (52%) identify themselves
as Republicans, though one-third (35%) identify as Independents. On the
other side of the class-culture divide, 49 percent of all Social Elites identify
as Democrats and 34 percent say they are Independents. It was said not so
long ago that conservatism was the ideology of the rich and privileged. Not
anymore. In the middle are the Disadvantaged, of whom half (51%) identify
as Independents, one-third (33%) identify as Democrats and only 16 percent
identify as Republicans.

As to who they would vote for, the results are mostly predictable. Seventy-four
percent of the Disinherited say if the election were held today, they would vote
for Trump, while 74 percent of Social Elites would vote for Clinton, with the
Disadvantaged favoring Clinton (52%) over Trump (28%) by nearly two to one.

What is striking in these findings are the numbers of Americans who will
vote for someone else or just not vote at all. For the Disadvantaged, the

figure is 20 percent while for both the Social Elite and the Disinherited, the figure is 12 percent.

The Candidates as Tribal Symbols

Social and cultural factors clearly predispose the American population toward sometimes starkly different political orientations. It also shows how clearly aligned the Disinherited and Social Elites are with the two candidates. But the findings of the *2016 Survey of American Political Culture* also suggest that the candidates themselves, in concert with the media, have a role in intensifying the political divisions. They crystallize political differences, not unlike a flag around whom supporters unite and act together. This dynamic may be especially important in a context where personalities loom large while political institutions (parties, special interest groups, etc.) fail to coalesce in coherent ways.

Thus, we see the stark differences noted at the start of this report:

- 77 percent of Trump supporters say they are in favor of "building a wall across the border between the US and Mexico," compared to 8 percent of Clinton supporters.

- 70 percent of all Trump supporters favor "banning entry to all Muslims until we better understand the threat to our country," compared to 82 percent of the Clinton supporters who oppose that policy.

- 85 percent of Trump supporters are in favor of "repealing the Affordable Care Act," while 73 percent of Clinton supporters oppose the idea.

- 79 percent of Clinton supporters agree that "if more Americans legally carried weapons in public," it would make our nation more dangerous, compared to 68 percent of all Trump supporters who say it would make the nation safer.

The differences continue:

- 77 percent of Trump supporters see the United States declining, while 75 percent of Clinton supporters see the nation holding steady or improving.

- 81 percent of Trump supporters have little to no confidence that the government in Washington can solve problems and 88 percent have little to no confidence that the people in our government tell the truth, compared to half of all Clinton supporters who have some or a lot of confidence on both points.

- 80 percent of all Trump supporters agree that the government in Washington threatens the freedom of ordinary Americans, compared to 61 percent of Clinton supporters who disagree with that statement.

- 82 percent of Clinton supporters favor increasing the tax rate on the wealthiest Americans, compared to 53 percent of Trump supporters who oppose that policy.

- 81 percent of Trump supporters disagree that the police and law enforcement unfairly target racial and ethnic minorities, compared to 65 percent of Clinton supporters who agree with that statement.

- 83 percent of Trump supporters agree that the United States has been too weak in dealing with other nations, compared to 68 percent of Clinton supporters who disagree with this view.

- 76 percent of Trump supporters favor greatly reducing the number of immigrants entering the United States, compared to 71 percent of Clinton supporters who oppose that policy.

- 88 percent of Clinton supporters say that immigrants strengthen our country because of their hard work and talents, compared to 52 percent of Trump supporters who say that immigrants are a burden on our country because they take away jobs, housing and health care.

- 73 percent of Clinton supporters favor requiring all areas of the country to officially permit gay marriage, compared to 61 percent of Trump supporters who oppose that policy.

- Almost all of Trump's supporters (93%) agree that "political correctness is a serious problem in our country, making it hard for people to say what they really think," compared to slightly over half (56%) of Clinton supporters who share that view.

- 70 percent of Clinton supporters agree that our founding fathers were part of a racist and sexist culture that gave important roles to white men while harming minorities and women, compared to 74 percent of Trump supporters who disagree.

Finally,

- 93 percent of Clinton supporters have a favorable view of Barack Obama, compared to 92 percent of Trump supporters who view him unfavorably.

Elections are always rituals of solidarity for competing political and ideological groups. Clearly, the candidates in the 2016 election have become potent symbols of different dispositions toward the world and different aspirations for its future. These dramatic differences point to the decline of a shared civic culture that provided a basis for compromise, set limits on partisan disagreements and made possible the broad governing consensus that historian Arthur Schlesinger, Jr., called the "vital center."

IV

AN AFTERWORD ON
LATE-STAGE DEMOCRACY

The 2016 presidential election has been widely viewed as an extraordinary event, something singular in the history of American presidential politics. This is undoubtedly true in certain respects. The findings of the *2016 Survey of American Political Culture*, however, tell a story that is probably more about continuity than it is about change.

Continuities

The continuities this survey reveals are now commonplace: The legitimation crisis of the last 50 years continues and, so far as we can tell, hardens as well. Many Americans are even more set in their view that government cannot be trusted; that its leaders (and the leadership class more broadly) are incompetent, craven and self-interested; and that, as citizens, they personally have little meaningful influence over the powerful institutions or circumstances that shape their lives.

Whatever else the culture war of the last four decades accomplished, it certainly contributed to the intensification of this legitimation crisis. What was seen as reasonable and justifiable governance by one side was viewed as irrational and indefensible by the other, and vice versa. Back and forth it went in political discourse that was less about persuasion than about denigrating the opposition through overstatement and hyperbole. The cycle has repeated itself over decades with great predictability on every issue under discussion: reproduction, immigration, education, issues of church and state, funding for the humanities and the arts, and so on. As it has borne on the presidency itself, we watched a toxic Clinton-hatred give way to an equally noxious Bush-hatred, which has more recently given way to an equally venomous Obama-hatred. This cycle will certainly continue into the future, regardless of who holds the executive office.

An antagonistic public discourse is hardly new in American history. What *is* new is the absence of a balance of thoughtful, political engagement by a seasoned and knowledgeable political class. What is also new is a media platform that favors the partisan over the nonpartisan, the sensational over the substantive, the superficial over the serious and the stupid over the sagacious. The relentless pursuit of ratings, market share and advertising dollars by the media establishment practically guarantee that it will continue to stoke a radically polarized, overheated and truncated public discourse well into the future.

Discursive strategies designed to debase opponents or opponents' arguments, used promiscuously for decades by both sides of the cultural divide and amplified by a powerful media industry more driven by entertainment value than truth, cannot be without long-term consequences. The deepening crisis of legitimacy for our governing philosophies, institutions and leaders is a natural consequence. But a more recent casualty is the idea that one can find any truth in the words of politicians and in the media, or that there is any realm of truth at all to be referenced when attempting to hold politicians, leaders and the media accountable.

A case in point is that nearly half of Trump's supporters (47%) actually question the birthright legitimacy of the Obama presidency while Clinton supporters reject this suggestion out of hand. How could this be? One explanation we can infer from the data is that competing sides of our political culture view the world in fundamentally different ways. How else can one explain Obama's favorability ratings? Superficially, the survey reveals a fairly even split between Americans who view Obama favorably and unfavorably. A balanced mix of opinions? Not exactly. On one side, only one of every twelve Trump supporters views Obama favorably, and on the other, only one of every fifteen Clinton supporters view Obama unfavorably. The lines of division are essentially tribal: Within the Trump and Clinton "tribes" the world is seen in different ways.

Yet what they share is the conviction that you can believe neither the politicians nor the media. Indeed, both Trump and Clinton supporters are equally and overwhelmingly likely to agree that "political events these days seem more like theater or entertainment than like something to be taken seriously." Truth, in the eyes of the general public, has become both malleable and manipulable.

The "vital center" of a hopeful and substantive liberal democracy, then, has all but disappeared, having been depleted through deliberate strategies of oppositional research, disparagement, and political theater that have become the stock and trade of consultants, special interest groups and political parties. It does not go too far to say that a discourse of negation — and the fear, animosity, distrust and lack of comprehension that it fosters — is the common culture of early twenty-first century American democracy.

It hasn't helped that the mediating institutions directly or indirectly charged with political formation — schools, youth organizations, churches and other institutions of faith, and local political parties — have weakened over the past half century. For many reasons not of their own making, these institutions have failed to cultivate the shared civic sensibility at the heart of citizenship. In the process, the shared civic dispositions that underwrote and therefore limited political disagreement have not been replenished. Neither has the civility, civic realism and idealism that accompanies vital democratic practice. To be sure, the Internet and social media have filled the gap, offering a certain kind of political community, along with a voice for many who were voiceless, but it is a weaker form of community, divided into enclaves and built on anonymous ties, with little more than virtual solidarity.

The credibility of the mainstream political establishment — its mission, governing authority and leaders — has taken a pounding over many years. After a half century of polling, one can say with near certainty that the confidence that average citizens have in their leaders and the governing institutions of American democracy have suffered blows that will continue to have lasting effects.

This is the story of continuity.

Change

There is something new here, however, though what is new is a consequence of conditions long in development. What is new are the levels of incoherence we find in our political institutions and their governing authority. On the one hand, the party establishments and their governing philosophies appear to be less meaningfully connected to the minds and hearts of their constituencies. This is reflected in the continuation of a long-term trend marked by growing numbers of self-identified Independents. But more significantly, leading candidates for the presidency have openly challenged or contradicted the ideas and rules of conduct that have long defined the mainstream party establishments. This was manifestly true in 2016 among Republicans for whom, under Trump, conservatism and party self-identification have been strained, if not severed. It was also true for Democrats, most notably in the surprisingly strong campaign of a candidate who didn't register as a Democrat until the day of the New Hampshire primary.

Also new are the economic changes that have become magnified in the public consciousness in the years following the Great Recession: underemployment, wage stagnation, the decline in certain areas of manufacturing, the loss of industry to developing parts of the world and the perceived loss of jobs through illegal immigration. While members of the professional and managerial upper middle class have seen their fortunes rise, the working and lower middle classes have suffered. The latter have seen the horizons of opportunity and hope for a better life grow more distant and, in some cases, disappear. What is more, they see many of the values and beliefs they live by — once perceived as honorable in their own communities — ridiculed as bigoted, homophobic, misogynist, xenophobic and backward by a privileged, powerful cultural elite. In the face of this onslaught, they have confronted the sting and personal humiliation of social "deplorability" long before Hillary Clinton spoke of such things during this election year.

In this light, the unusual candidacies of Donald Trump, Bernie Sanders, Ted Cruz and others are not so much anomalous as they are reflections of the political confusion of our times which has not been addressed coherently and effectively by the political establishment and its leaders. Moreover, the soft authoritarian appeal of some of the recent candidates holds a growing attraction because it promises clarity in the face of murkiness and strong, effective leadership in the face of inept or corrupt leadership. It doesn't matter whether the champions of such promises can deliver on their claims; it is the promise that counts. If Trump didn't exist, some might say, we would have to invent him.

The 2016 presidential election was the stage upon which these deeper, longer-term cultural and institutional dynamics are being played out: The 2016 race pitted a weakening political establishment (that happened to be Democratic) against an emerging populist insurgency (that happened to be Republican). It just as easily could have been the other way. Authoritarian impulses bubble up from the Right and the Left.

In short, as long as the social, cultural and political conditions described above are in place, we are likely to see more election years like 2016, with similar campaigns and candidates.

Democracy as Form and Substance

What all of this portends is open for debate. The form of American democracy — the rituals of a primary season, of nominating candidates, of debate and so on — is fairly sturdy, and that sturdiness gives democracy the appearance of vitality. But underneath and within that sturdy frame is the substance of democracy, which, at its best, is constituted by high-minded ideals, rich governing philosophies, capable leaders who give fresh voice to those ideals, practices of civility in the face of bitter disagreement, and a knowledgeable and virtuous citizenry. The substance has not disappeared, but there is no question that it has been depleted — to the point, some would say, of being all but hollowed out.

Does the 2016 election signify a tipping point? We will know only in retrospect. American democracy has never fully embodied its ideals in the past and it will never fully do so in the future. But there are darker alternatives that seem more visible and foreboding than we have seen in a while. The cultural conditions that have made those alternatives plausible will likely be with us for some time to come.

APPENDIX

Survey Questionnaire with Percentage Distributions of Response

*All numbers are weighted percentage of response. Figures do not always add up to
100 percent due to rounding. The data is available electronically at www.iasc-culture.org/
research/publications/vanishing-center*

1. When the government in Washington decides to solve a problem, how
    much confidence do you have that the problem will actually be solved?

    - 6 A lot
    - 30 Some
    - 34 Just a little
    - 29 None at all

2. How much confidence do you have in the people who run our
    government to tell the truth to the public?

    - 6 A lot
    - 28 Some
    - 36 Just a little
    - 31 None at all

3. In general, how much confidence do you have in the wisdom of the
    American people when it comes to electing their national leaders?

    - 9 A lot
    - 38 Some
    - 39 Just a little
    - 15 None at all

4. Which of the following comes closest to your view of the United States?

> 47 The U.S. is the greatest country in the world,
>   better than all other countries
> 43 The U.S. is a great country, but so are certain other countries
> 10 There are some other countries that are better than the U.S.

5. How patriotic would you say that you are?

> 2 Not patriotic at all
> 5 Not very patriotic
> 36 Moderately patriotic
> 57 Very patriotic

6. How much change do you think we need in our American system of government? Would you say...

> 9 The system is good and needs very little change
> 33 The system is fine, but the people running it need to be changed
> 46 Major changes are needed in both the
>   system and the people running it
> 12 The system of government itself is broken and needs
>   to be replaced with something completely different

7. If we had a President you really believed in and trusted, would you want the President's actions to be limited by Congress and the Courts, as they are now, or would you want the President authorized to enact his or her agenda even if Congress did not support it?

> 81 His or her actions should be limited as they are now
> 19 He or she should be authorized to act
>   without Congressional support

8. In general, do you think the United States is in a decline as a nation, are we holding steady, or is the nation improving?

> 25 Strongly declining
> 23 Moderately declining
> 33 Holding steady
> 15 Moderately improving
> 4 Strongly improving

9. Would you say people like you are doing much better, better, about the same, worse, or much worse than twenty-five years ago?

    10 Much better
    27 Better
    27 About the same
    26 Worse
    10 Much worse

10. Twenty-five years from now, do you think the future for people like you will be much better, better, about the same, worse, or much worse than life today?

    9   Much better
    28 Better
    28 About the same
    25 Worse
    10 Much worse

11. Thinking about your family's current financial situation, would you say you are currently in excellent financial shape, good shape, only fair shape, or in poor shape financially?

    9   Excellent
    42 Good
    36 Only fair
    13 Poor

12. Americans have recently voiced a variety of objections about our economy, politics, and the government. For each of the following, please tell me whether you completely agree, mostly agree, mostly disagree, or completely disagree with the complaint.

	Completely Agree	Mostly Agree	Mostly Disagree	Completely Disagree
Our economic system is rigged in favor of the wealthiest Americans	31	42	20	7
Our system of government is good, but the people running it are incompetent	29	42	23	6
The most educated and successful people in America are more interested in serving themselves than in serving the common good	21	40	30	8
You can't believe much of what you hear from the mainstream media	40	35	20	5
Wall Street and big businesses in our country often profit at the expense of ordinary Americans	40	44	13	4
These days, I feel like a stranger in my own country	14	24	35	27
The best government is the one that governs the least	21	38	31	10
What Americans really need is a new political party because the current two-party system isn't working	29	34	25	12
Political events these days seem more like theater or entertainment than like something to be taken seriously	45	43	9	3
Most politicians are more interested in winning elections than in doing what is right	47	43	9	2
The leaders in American corporations, media, universities, and technology care little about the lives of most Americans	19	43	31	6

13. Now I want you to consider some additional things some people are saying about our country. For each one, please tell me whether you completely agree, mostly agree, mostly disagree, or completely disagree with the complaint.

	Completely Agree	Mostly Agree	Mostly Disagree	Completely Disagree
Most Americans who live in poverty are there because of their own bad choices and habits	9	28	40	23
Most elected officials don't care what people like me think	28	46	22	4
I am proud to live under our American system of government	38	46	12	3
America should pursue its own agenda even when its allies don't agree	22	40	29	9
America is an exceptional nation with a special responsibility to lead the world	35	46	15	4
The United States has been too weak in dealing with other nations	25	29	33	13
These days, the government in Washington threatens the freedom of ordinary Americans	22	34	29	15
Political correctness is a serious problem in our country, making it hard for people to say what they really think	40	33	17	10
We need a President who will completely change the direction of this country	40	32	20	8
Our founding fathers were part of a racist and sexist culture that gave important roles to white men while harming minorities and women	19	33	25	23
People like me don't have any say in what the government does	26	38	25	11
The American way of life is rapidly disappearing	24	34	30	12

	Completely Agree	Mostly Agree	Mostly Disagree	Completely Disagree
People of other races can't really understand how my race sees things	12	32	37	18
The police and law enforcement unfairly target racial and ethnic minorities	18	27	32	23
Most Americans vote without really thinking through the issues	38	48	11	3
America used to be a place where you could get ahead by working hard, but this is no longer true	26	33	28	12
If you follow the rules and behave responsibly, you can pretty much expect life will turn out well	20	51	21	8

14. I'm going to read you some pairs of statements. As I read each pair, tell me whether the FIRST statement or the SECOND statement comes closer to your own views — even if neither is exactly right.

	Percent Who Agree
Americans who want to get ahead can make it if they're willing to work hard, OR	59
Hard work and determination are no guarantee of success for most Americans	41
Government should do more to improve the lives of ordinary Americans, OR	52
Government is doing too many things better left to businesses, civic groups, and individuals	48
Immigrants strengthen our country because of their hard work and talents, OR	71
Immigrants are a burden on our country who take jobs, housing, and health care	29

15. Now, I'm going to read you some proposals that are being discussed nationally. Do you strongly favor, favor, oppose, or strongly oppose each policy?

	Strongly Favor	Favor	Oppose	Strongly Oppose
Building a wall across the border between the U.S. and Mexico	18	15	25	42
Banning entry to all Muslims until we better understand the terrorist threat to our country	20	18	31	31
Increasing the tax rate on the wealthiest Americans	36	32	20	12
Requiring all areas of the country to officially permit gay marriage	32	28	20	20
Repealing the Affordable Care Act, sometimes called Obamacare	33	19	24	24
Greatly reducing the number of immigrants entering the United States	20	29	32	19

16. If more Americans legally carried weapons in public, do you think it would make our nation much safer, somewhat safer, somewhat more dangerous, or much more dangerous, or do you think it would have no effect upon our public safety?

    16 Much safer
    19 Somewhat safer
    18 Somewhat more dangerous
    34 Much more dangerous
    14 No real effect

17. Looking back over the last ten years, do you think the quality of life for your racial or ethnic group in the US has gotten better, stayed about the same, or gotten worse?

    19 Better
    49 Same
    32 Worse

18. For the following groups, do you see their beliefs and values as being completely different, mostly different, mostly similar, or completely the same as Americans like you?

	Completely Different	Mostly Different	Mostly Similar	Completely The Same
African Americans	8	22	54	15
Hispanic Americans	7	19	60	14
White Americans	5	14	58	24
Muslim or Islamic Americans	23	35	34	8
Conservative Christians	12	25	46	16
Non-religious people	15	26	44	15
Gays and lesbians	17	24	45	14
America's cultural elite	25	40	27	7
The wealthiest 10% of Americans	33	37	23	7

19. Now we'd like your views on some political leaders. Would you say your overall opinion of [name] is very favorable, mostly favorable, mostly unfavorable, or very unfavorable?

	Very Favorable	Mostly Favorable	Mostly Unfavorable	Very Unfavorable
Hillary Clinton	13	30	23	35
Donald Trump	9	21	24	46
Barack Obama	26	30	21	23
Bernie Sanders	19	40	24	17

20. Do you believe that Barack Obama was born in the United States, or not?

    75 Yes

    21 No

     2 Probably yes (volunteered)

     1 Probably no (volunteered)

21. Generally speaking, do you usually think of yourself as a Republican, a Democrat, an Independent, or what?

    26 A Republican
    31 A Democrat
    42 An independent
    1 Other (volunteered)

22. [If a Republican or Democrat]: How well do you believe [your party] as it exists today represents your own views of how the government should operate?

    15 Republican; well-represented
    11 Republican; not well-represented
    25 Democrat; well-represented
    7 Democrat; not well-represented
    42 Independent

23. Which of the following best describes your overall political beliefs?

    13 Very conservative
    23 Somewhat conservative
    33 Moderate
    18 Somewhat liberal
    12 Very liberal

24. How likely is it that you will vote in the 2016 election for President this November? Would you say you will definitely vote, probably vote, probably not vote, or definitely not vote?

    75 Definitely vote
    12 Probably vote
    6 Probably not vote
    7 Definitely not vote

25. If the Presidential election were being held today between Hillary Clinton, the Democrat, and Donald Trump, the Republican, who would you vote for?

    51 Hillary Clinton
    36 Donald Trump
     8 Someone else (volunteered)
     5 Wouldn't vote (volunteered)

26. For each of the following statements, please tell me if you completely agree, mostly agree, mostly disagree, or completely disagree.

	Completely agree	Mostly agree	Mostly disagree	Completely disagree
We should be more tolerant of people who adopt alternate lifestyles	39	48	10	4
All views of what is good are equally valid	17	47	24	11
Everything is beautiful; it's all a matter of how you look at it	25	45	22	9
Some things are absolutely right and wrong, whether or not people can see it or recognize it	44	43	11	2
We would all be better off if we could live by the same basic moral guidelines	36	46	13	5
In general, Americans lived more moral and ethical lives 50 years ago	34	34	23	9

27. What is your religious preference, if any?

    68 Christian
     2 Jewish
     1 Muslim
     8 Other
    21 None

28. (If Christian) Are you Catholic, or not?

    27 Yes, Catholic
    72 No, not Catholic
    <1 Grew up Catholic, but no longer associated
        with Catholics (volunteered)

29. (If Christian) Some people think of themselves as Evangelical or
    born-again Christians. Do you ever think of yourself as an Evangelical
    or born-again Christian, or not?

    36 Yes
    64 No

30. How important to you are your religious beliefs?

    10 Not at all important
    11 Not too important
    20 Fairly important
    35 Very important
    24 The most important thing in my life

31. Which word best describes your religious beliefs or orientation?

    14 Very conservative
    24 Conservative
    36 Moderate
    15 Liberal
    12 Very liberal

32. How often do you pray — daily, several times a week, once a week,
    2 or 3 times a month, once a month or less, or never?

    49 Daily
    15 Several times a week
     7 Once a week
     5 2 or 3 times a month
     9 Once a month or less
    15 Never

33. What is your gender?

    50 Male
    50 Female
    <1 Other/Trans (volunteered)

34. Please tell me your age

    29 18-34
    25 35-49
    26 50-64
    20 65+

35. What is the highest level of school you have completed or the highest degree you have received?

    9 Less than a high school diploma
    32 High school graduate
    2 Technical, trade, vocational or business school or program after high school
    18 Some college — college, university, or community college — but no degree
    9 Two-year associate degree from a college, university, or community college
    19 Four year bachelor's degree from a college or university
    1 Some postgraduate or professional schooling after graduating college, but no postgraduate degree
    8 Master's degree
    3 Other postgraduate or professional degree, including Ph.D.

36. Which of the following best describes your total annual household income before taxes?

    9 Under $15,000
    13 $15,000 to less than $25,000
    24 $25,000 to less than $50,000
    19 $50,000 to less than $75,000
    13 $75,000 to less than $100,000
    18 $100,000 to less than $250,000
    3 $250,000 to less than $500,000
    1 $500,000 or more

37. Are you of Hispanic, Latino, or Spanish origin — such as Mexican,
   Puerto Rican, Cuban, or other Spanish origin?

   16 Yes
   84 No

38. Which of the following best describes your race? (Combined with
   Hispanic ethnicity data)

   72 White non-Hispanic
   12 Hispanic
   12 Black non-Hispanic
    1 Asian
    2 Other

39. What is your own current marital status?

   27 Never married
   53 Now married
    3 Separated
   11 Divorced
    6 Widowed